BRIDPORT PRIZE 202

EXTRACTS FROM THE N

JUDGE
Sarah Hall

First published in 2023 by Redcliffe Press Ltd
81g Pembroke Road, Bristol BS8 3EA

e: info@redcliffepress.co.uk
www.redcliffepress.co.uk
Follow us on Twitter @RedcliffePress

© the contributors

Follow The Bridport Prize:
Follow us on Twitter and Instagram @BridportPrize
www.bridportprize.org.uk
www.facebook.com/bridportprize

ISBN 978-1-915670-10-6

British Library Cataloguing-in-Publication Data
A catalogue record for this book is available from the British Library

All rights reserved. Except for the purpose of review, no part of this book may be reproduced, stored in a retrieval system, or transmitted, in any form or by any means, electronic, mechanical, photocopying, recording or otherwise, without the prior permission of the publishers.

Typeset in 10.5pt Times

Typeset by Addison Print Ltd, Northampton
Printed by Hobbs the Printers Ltd, Totton

Contents

Introduction	5
Novel Award Partners	7
Judge's Report	9
The Origins of Poppies Jilly Carrell	11
Fly Catcher P C Cubitt	18
I Just Live Here Pauline Diamond Salim RUNNER-UP	25
Paradise Beach Lucy Foster FIRST PRIZE	32
The Ties that Bind Us Faiza Hasan HIGHLY COMMENDED	38
The Sunlit Pool of the Finished Image David Hill	45
Pretzel Hilary Hudgins	51
A Scrape of Patience Angela Hunter	58
The Chameleon Bush Tony Irvin	64
Run As If The Devil Were After You Jenny Jack HIGHLY COMMENDED	72
Bem's Dream War is Two Centimetres Dilated SallyAnne Khan	79
Love, I must go Rebekah Miron HIGHLY COMMENDED, DORSET PRIZE	85
HuKaMa (Brotherhood) Murungu	90
Wolnam Yoanna Pak	98
Lazarus in Heels Susan Perry	104
Martha Dunn Caroline Price	110
Migratory Patterns Margaret Sessa-Hawkins	116
Small Thief Liz Skitt	123
Exit Interview Isabel Tejera	131
Somewhere to Go Gwen Williams	138
Biographies	144

Writing human

Opening the cover, reading the first page, a book is about possibilities. It's meeting new people in places full of emotion. You're never alone.

Writing a book is a different story. A single idea turns into a rollercoaster of thoughts: how to start, when to end. Publication is a dream until it actually happens, then it feels like a dream. Seeing your novel in a bookshop is life affirming.

The writers in this anthology kept going through word shortages and editing feasts. Having never written a novel, they threaded together characters, plots and the dreaded synopsis.

It worked. We're proud to publish our finalists and winners. As you travel with them, we hope you gain insight and inspiration.

Our new honorary patron and best-selling author, Kit de Waal did not begin writing till her mid 50s: 'I've been on the receiving end of the Prize a couple of times and know how prizes can change your writing life – not just the winners but everyone who enters and strives to get their work good enough to enter.'

Kit is living proof it's never too late to write.

Without stories we are all less human. AI we are watching you!

The Bridport Prize Team

Where are they now? Our top ten

Colin Walsh
Highly Commended for his short story in 2017, Colin's 'landmark' debut novel, *Kala* was published this summer. It's Atlantic Books first ever super lead title after they acquired the book in a five way auction.

Fiona Williams
Fiona won with us in 2021 with her novel, *The House of Broken Bricks*, shortly to be Faber's 'heart catching' debut super lead in January 2024. Fiona says 'winning opened doors I didn't know existed.'

David Swann
A frequent Bridport Prize winner across genres, David's novella, *Season of Bright Sorrow* recently published by Ad Hoc Press has been named international Rubery Book of the Year.

Julia Rampen
Runner up for her novel in 2020, *The Bay* was published this summer. Julia is represented by Euan Thorneycroft of AM Heath Literary Agency, our novel partner.

Wenyan Lu
Longlisted for her novel in 2019, Wenyan's debut novel *The Funeral Cryer* was published by Allen & Unwin in spring this year. She says, 'It has always been my dream to see my novel on the bookshelves.'

Sean Lusk
Runner up in our short story competition in 2014, Sean went onto great success with his 2022 debut novel *The Second Sight of Zachary Cloudesley,* which was shortlisted for the Scottish National Book awards debut of the year and longlisted for the Walter Scott Prize for historical fiction.

Carla Jenkins
Longlisted in 2020, Carla's debut novel *Fifty Minutes* will be published by Hachette as one of their key titles in May 2024, with her second novel due for publication the year after.

Carole Hailey
Highly commended in 2020, Carole's novel *The Silence Project* was published in February 2023 and chosen for Radio 2's Book Club. Carol says, 'being longlisted then shortlisted for the Bridport Prize was so important for both me and *The Silence Project!*'

Lara Haworth
Highly commended for her short story in 2022 adapted from her draft novel *Monumenta,* Canongate are publishing *Monumenta* next summer.

Catherine Chidgey
A 2018 winner and longlisted for the Women's Prize for Fiction, Catherine's novels have achieved international acclaim. The *New York Times* described her latest novel *Pet* as 'a landmark in the small but potent canon of contemporary novels about unusual girls reckoning with themselves and the world.'

Novel Award Partners

The Bridport Prize is proud to work in partnership with the following organisations in the delivery of the Peggy Chapman-Andrews Award for a First Novel.

A.M. Heath Literary Agents
Founded in 1919 by Audrey Heath and Alice May Spinks, two women who challenged the conventions of publishing, we are a London literary agency still very much driven by a passion to help writers who want to shift, shape or enrich the wider cultural conversation, and provide irresistible entertainment.

Championing our clients' writing remains at the heart of what we do. As well as a century of experience, we bring energy, ambition, and a keen eye for detail to our work.

We're always looking out for original ideas combined with great quality writing, and we work with the Bridport Prize to encourage emerging writers. By helping to draw up the long-list and shortlist for the Peggy Chapman-Andrews Award for a First Novel, we aim to support the best new novelists to find publishers and readers across the world.

Website: www.amheath.com
Twitter: @EuanThorneycrof / @AMHeathLtd

Headline Fiction
Headline Fiction is a place that prides itself on understanding readers, what drives them to buy and read books and where and how they read them. Our authors are at the heart of everything we do, and our aim is to nurture their writing, and to build careers that will endure. We publish books that win prizes, reach millions of readers internationally, and top charts.

Our reach is broad, encompassing several imprints and some of the best (and bestselling) storytellers in the business. From the extraordinary tales of Neil Gaiman to Maggie O'Farrell's rich prize-winners, breakout debut voices like Bolu Babalola and Bobby Palmer to the spellbinding worlds of Deborah Harkness and Octavia E. Butler, we publish the novels that people really want to read – the books that keep them reading into the early hours, with worlds that people want to escape to and characters they can relate to.

Website: www.headline.co.uk
Facebook: /headlinebooks/
Instagram: @headlinebooks

The Literary Consultancy
The Literary Consultancy is the UK's first and leading writing consultancy, offering editorial services since 1996. Its aim is to provide honest, professional feedback to writers to give them a better sense of whether and where their work might fit into the ever-changing market.

TLC and its team of world-class professional editors work with writers writing in English at all levels, across all genres. Its most popular services include manuscript assessment, developmental editing, submission package reports, and one-to-one mentoring. It is also home to Being A Writer, a membership platform for writers who want to create happier, healthier writing habits.

TLC meets writers on the page. Its services and resources equip writers with the context, confidence, and skills they need to thrive and flourish.

Email: info@literaryconsultancy.co.uk
Website: literaryconsultancy.co.uk
Twitter: @TLCUK
Facebook: The Literary Consultancy

SARAH HALL

Judge's Report

The first prize winner, *Paradise Beach*. It is wonderful for a piece of fiction to transport and relocate the reader to another setting, and one of the immediate joys of this novel is its nuanced, colourful, intimate depiction of Santa María, the coastal margins, and Mexico City. As a reader I always want to know and experience the exact world I'm entering, how it looks and operates, how feels; I want to be convinced, cerebrally and sensually, of the geography, the people, cuisine, customs, politics, weather, and the layers of history. The atoms and dynamism of a place, through which it is evoked and activated in the imagination. If a writer constructs a convincing virtual reality, an artful frame for narratives, the characters and dramas within make more sense.

Paradise Beach is brilliant in this regard, with superb details of physical setting – the seaside houses, of both the rich and poor, drowned graveyards, big weather, streets and vibrant sunsets, mountains and rivers. It's brilliant too in its astute understanding of the residents and visitors who populate both the marginal spaces and the tremendous, brutal, fizzing metropolis of the city.

The portraiture and development of the characters is deft and compelling, with the dancing apart and weaving together of protagonists, as the tragic plot of a dead child and a missing mother begins to gain momentum and intrigue. They move, not as predetermined pieces in service to a story-board, but as flawed, empathic, reactive human beings through their unfolding fates. We can feel the presence of powerful, malevolent forces – an underbelly of criminality and dark economy in the region – presiding over the story, and the multicultural heart of the country itself. But it is these ordinary individuals who really illuminate the canvas, who illustrate the complicated, stratified nature of the place, with all its hardship, opportunity, chaos, verve, beauty and tenacity. Its spirit.

And spirit is really caught within the writing style, which is by turns worldly, confronting, poetic, and flavourful. It's rare to find an author who is like a conduit, who – this reader certainly feels – could take us to many other places too, just as vividly and as skilfully. Rarer still to find an author capable of level observation, and so capable of reproducing humanity's dissonance, its joys and heartaches, its ironies and truths.

The runner-up is *I Just Live Here*. Spanning several generations of a family, and several eras in Glasgow, this novel cleverly lays down the mystery of missing paintings after the death of a celebrated, reclusive artist. The story is told from the perspective of several women - either directly involved with the man himself, or in the aftermath of his death - to create a lovely, refractive, composite piece of fiction that reveals hidden aspects of both the characters and the world in which they live.

The writer carefully develops the relationships in the book, between mother and daughter, artist and lover, auctioneer and art industry, and explores our notions of value and worth - both material and emotional - asking what we cherish most and why, and when we might act improperly to preserve integrity or keep those we love close by. It's a lovely, calibrated novel, that moves through time and the city using interesting angles and optics. The depictions of both old and modern Glasgow are faceted and atmospheric, from the poorer classes to the gentrification of tenements. At the heart of the book is the idea of versions of reality, versions of identity, and from the varying narrative perspectives the reader comes to understand that, like art, much of life, and much of our behaviour, is open to interpretation.

The Highly Commended novels are *Love, I Must Go* which illuminates a single night in a woman's life as she decides to leave her husband. Through clever flashback and in deft prose, the author expands and collapses an entire life. This quietly compelling novella has a strong emotional undertow, and I was enthralled by it.

Run As If The Devil Were After You is a thrilling, evocative tale of a woman grappling with the 7 year old mystery of her sister's disappearance. Driven by unresolved grief and the garbled clues from a psychiatric patient at the hospital where she works, Gwen Merrick pursues her sister's memory deep into the past, until the present catches up with her.

The Ties That Bind Us is an unflinching, sensory drama about the Harding family, an estranged mother and daughter pulled into close quarters when one is diagnosed with a degenerative illness. Through the language of love, resentment and food, the novel explores themes of motherhood, inheritance and bodily autonomy – and the quiet traumas that echo across the generations of a family.

JILLY CARRELL

The Origins of Poppies

Synopsis
The Origins of Poppies *is an auto-fictional novel based on the writer's experiences as a contemporary military wife living through fifteen years of the Afghan conflict. The themes of motherhood, war, betrayal, grief, and the presence and absence of love are explored. We learn through the course of the book that the real trauma of military life happens at home.*

Eliza is married to Jack, a dominant army officer, and is the mother of their two daughters, Sylvie and Kitty. Her identity is eroded due to the requirements of one of the last bastions of the British class system. The Army, as well as her husband's and society's expectations of her, are exhaustive. She lives her life in negotiation between her husband's presence and absence and society's expectations of her as the feminine carer of a masculine hero.

The impact of Jack's repeat deployments to Afghanistan on his character, their marriage, and their children's lives forces Eliza to contemplate her role as a woman, wife, and mother living close to a morally ambiguous war. Towards the end of his army career, she faces her husband's catastrophic personal choices, Covid 19 and lockdown and his terminal cancer diagnosis and death.

This is the story of a wife obscured by her husband and the military machine which consumes him. It questions the heroism of soldiering. It aims to give flesh and complexity to a woman whose depth of story and diversity of character is often stifled by the pursuit of his army career and the acclaim it brings to him.

Prologue
Repatriation
June 2009, RAF Lyneham, Wiltshire
The repatriation party assembles in the welfare office, and the rain beats a farewell drum on the corrugated prefab roof. Eliza's coat is soaked through, and her black woollen sweater clings to her like a dead sheep to a hillside. The leaden clouds obscure until the final moment, the Hercules descending from Hell, as the water sheers off the fuselage of the soldiers' tomb. Vapours of grief and aviation fuel hang in the air.

Eliza stands apart from the waiting others, she wishes she were invisible, but her discomfort is transparent. She has no place at this ceremony of brutal unhusbanding, yet the Army has ordered that she be here, and Jack, too, insists it's her duty.

The Families' Room at RAF Lyneham is stark with Army-issue furniture in a miserable orange teak. Bruised steel filing cabinets line the walls, and someone, probably a welfare clerk, has placed some faded silk flowers in a chipped jug in an attempt to humanise the military machine, part of some policy directive written by the soul-less in Whitehall.

An ambush of widows stands apart from the other corralled together but standing apart on the other side of the room. Her friend Jenny is amongst them, her dark head bent, her lank hair falling into her eyes, and her arms wrapped tightly around her usually frenetic, wiry body. Now she's ominously still. She's wearing Kev's army ski fleece; the sleeves are too long and hang over her hands. Her jeans have dirty patches on the knees, and the lace of one of her red Converse trainers, a trademark of Jenny's energy and light, gapes open and trails across the floor.

Kev was blown up in Babaji on Thursday when one son was learning his letters and sounds, and the smallest was learning to eat solids in his highchair. The pieces of Kev's body are coming home in a bag.

"You can't be friends with other ranks wives," Jack had told Eliza back on that first day the two women had met.

"It's just not done, Lize." Jack had been resolute, but so had Eliza.

She'd been at the Army community centre, a three-month Sylvie pink and swaddled inside her pram. Eliza had been immediately struck by Jenny's vitality and the thrum of energy around her, in contrast to the dismal surroundings of the Army patch.

Eliza had ignored Jack, and Jenny had become her only friend on that military camp, her first posting as an army wife.

She doesn't try to catch Jenny's eye or approach her now. Neither of them will be able to stomach the usual platitudes. Instead, Eliza focuses on the comforting pain in the burning balls of her feet from the pinching black heels she only wears for mess balls and funerals. The damp seeps through the carpet, foaming at the edges with fragile rainbow bubbles.

Jack's whole frame is taut with respect, arms straight as bayonets, and his fingers curled into dutiful fists. He doesn't look at her or the widows, and she knows that in his mind, even a shard of emotion, an expression of his sympathy would render him complicit.

After seven months of patrolling the green zone of Helmand Province, Afghanistan, six men of B Company are coming home two weeks early and a lifetime too soon. They'd had two short weeks of R&R, coming

The Origins of Poppies

home with the fine sand of the Dasht-e Margo, a desert of solonchaks and takirs spilling out of their desert combats, an old-fashioned egg timer on their kitchen floors. Homecoming banners have already been made, and dyed bedsheets are covered in glitter.

Welcome Home from Afghanistan, Daddy.

A beautiful and terrible thing.

Eliza is startled by the leather-gloved hand on her shoulder, urgently tapping her into focus.

"It's time, ma'am," a young officer says to her in clipped tones, his bubble-gum face too close to hers. It's a command rather than a request, the grave formality of this day a perverse thrill to him, a validation of his years of training, duty, and calling.

"Don't tap me. I know what's expected of me, thanks." Eliza shrugs away the fingers on her arm and turns her face away from him, making no attempt to follow him or do as he says.

She doesn't know what she's expected to do, but today, she has no appetite for being corralled by some fresh-faced Sub-Lieutenant. She doesn't want to be rude but, incarcerated in this hut, imprisoned by this day, she has nowhere to go with the complexity of her feelings. He struts back to Jack, his superior officer, but his glove indicates it's time to mobilise towards the runway, where Union flag-covered coffins will soon be unloaded from the Herc. Jack's expression is professional and unreadable, but the tick under his eye gives him away to Eliza anyway. He checks his watch and scans the clouds west of the building. He's bareheaded as protocol dictates and pauses, allowing the women and their assigned visiting officers to filter through the aluminium doors ahead of him, their black umbrellas puncturing the grey landscape.

The bearer party officers leap to attention through the open door at the side of the runway. One is holding a bugle; he's young, and his acne is inflamed. Eliza worries he might pass out as he sways on his heels, back and forth, gaining dangerous momentum like a metronome.

As Jenny begins to make her way outside, something propels Eliza forward, and she grabs her hand. She squeezes it, and their fingers interlace in an intimate and yet somehow grotesque gesture of togetherness, a shared experience indescribable to those on the outside. Something passes between them – an acknowledgement of Jenny's sacrifice and their years of subjugation and pain at the hands of the military machine. Then Jenny is ushered forward by Jack, and Eliza is forced to release her grip on Jenny. The bugle screeches in a false start.

Eliza has never despised Jack more than at this moment. He stands in the doorway of the prefab, his fingers drumming on the metal frame.

"Come on, hurry up." He beckons Eliza towards him. Her reticence smacks of insubordination.

"No," she says simply, "I won't."

She's weary of being his strength and stay, doing as she's told in a false show of solidarity and duty. She's tired of putting the needs of the service first in the mantra of their marriage. Jack reddens and beckons again, more peevish and aggravated, as he can't raise his voice to her in front of his soldiers. His face darkens, and she knows she'll pay for this later. He lets the door slam behind him as he marches towards his soldiers. The repatriation is underway, and the wails of the wind and the women are a siren's shriek through the asbestos walls.

Eliza is alone now. The air around her is disturbed. She puts in her headphones, turns the music up loud, and is grateful when it devours her.

Chapter 1
The World of After
2001, Edinburgh

Eliza returned to Edinburgh after fifteen years of London's bright lights and burdensome beauty. Her hometown and its changing skies, sudden vistas and the smell of the malty sea has always had the power to heal.

She burns up her paltry savings on the deposit for a small light flat on the top floor of a Georgian tenement. She buys an old leather armchair from the junk shop round the corner and shoehorns it into the narrow bay of her bedroom window. She's on the fourth floor, which looks out across the Craigleith sandstone and the hex brown rooftops. For the first time in years, Eliza is at ease with herself, wrapped in an old crochet blanket; her view is perfectly obscured by the high branches of the billowing cherry blossom from the trees of the tiny walled garden planted into the cobbles below. The orchard blooms late, its perfume heavy with hope. Still, she has no regrets about her old life, her burnt-out corporate self and the identikit lovers she's left behind. She shares her life with Cynthia, her ageing rescue cat. They share cold boiled eggs and all-night electric blankets on low and listen to Radio Four until the shipping forecast bids them goodnight, warning of gales in Fair Isle and Viking. She feels content in her bed, deep within the fog-wrapped evenings of a reluctant Spring.

Eliza is in no rush to fire-start her career again, preferring the pace of this capital city to the last. She takes a job in the West End as a media manager in Drummonds, a small firm of solicitors whose pace is slow and hypnotic, and the employees down tools in daily collegiate togetherness for mid-morning tea and shortbread biscuits. She spends her days writing soporific press releases for the local news, drafting statements for the partners and framing their views on minor technical changes to the law and order of the City.

Her Saturdays are occupied with trips to art galleries and street food safaris; her favourite local delicacy is an oatmeal pudding deep fried and drenched in runny brown vinegar sauce. She buys novels from a labyrinthic bookshop in the Cowgate and trudges down Leith Walk to the real pubs with steam-dripped windows. She stops periodically to inhale the beauty of the Old Town and the sea, cold as a witch's breath and embraces the thrill of being alone. She has a few friends, but only a few. She visits the cinema or Rick's Bar for Martini Thursdays with them, and their relations are uncomplicated. Sometimes, there's a guy in a bar, and they fuck, and he gives her a number, but she never calls because nothing sticks, and she doesn't want it to.

Jack marches into her life as a keynote speaker at a work seminar during this untethered existence. She's doodling in the agenda section of her Filofax when he takes the stage to present.

"Good morning, ladies and gentlemen; thank you for being here today."

The boom in his voice startles her, and she stops doodling, the hungover lines of her pen merging and swirling. She's hungover and irritated. The room is silent, waiting for the pin to drop, and all eyes focus on the military uniform standing on the platform. The man at the podium is a broad-shouldered action man whose shoulders are square, not rounded like those of her desk-bound colleagues. His dark hair is swept back from his olive skin. The sleeves of his uniform shirt are folded back, exposing the dense hairs on his forearms. A pen is entwined between his middle and forefinger; he pauses and twirls it like a wand, releasing secrets and truths, or lies, to the audience. The movement is hypnotic. He's got the room.

He's not her type, Eliza thinks, appraising him out of habit rather than desire. He's too obvious, with his square jaw and arms folded across his chest, legs planted firmly apart. His confidence radiates, carried by his charismatic, uncomplicated manner and easy smile. His voice soothes, rather than excites her for the next thirty minutes, and she absorbs nothing of what he says, the sound of him proving to be more of a lullaby than a call to action.

He finishes his set on *How to be a leader of men (and women) and still be 'Nice'* and spies the empty seat beside Eliza. It doesn't take him long to realise that the woman in the seat beside him is nauseous and irritable. He winks at her when she groans, her head thumping as she exhales Martini fumes from every pore. Maybe he spots an opportunity, or perhaps he's just the nice person his PowerPoint says he is. Still, he rummages around in his canvas rucksack and presents her with a sweaty clingfilm package containing a fat doorstep sandwich.

"Take this," he says firmly, "You'll feel better if you eat something."

"Thank you, honestly, no, it's OK, I'm fine," she hesitates.

Her face flushes with irritation at being rumbled by this smooth prick in a uniform. She swallows bile and leans back in her seat, shutting her eyes and tuning out the Captain and his shiny annoying face. She opens her eyes after a moment, conscious of her unfriendly tone, and he's still smiling, extending the sandwich from his upturned palm. She attempts a sideways glance at him, embarrassed by her vulnerability, unsure how to play this. Jack smiles and, ignoring the tremble in her hands, hands her the yellowing plastic cup from the top of his small thermos of coffee to wash down the sandwich. He grins at her, pleased. Something shifts within Eliza. He's regimented and too public school for her; he's not her type, but his kindness is unexpected, and the vodka distilling in her veins makes her vulnerable, so she takes the cup and gulps back the scalding liquid.

When the conference breaks for lunch, after what seems like a decade, Jack offers to escort Eliza to the adjacent blustery Princes Street Gardens for fresh air and more caffeine.

"I can bore you with my war stories and charm. Come on; I won't take no for an answer," he says, jokingly but determined.

"Do you always get what you want?" Eliza asks, both annoyed and, despite herself, slightly intrigued. She pulls on the leather jacket she'd bought on Saturday, perfect for a night out but less than ideal for a stroll through the gale force winds now whistling through the city streets.

He raises his eyebrows, and lines appear across his forehead as he considers her questions. He runs his fingers through his fringe, pushing his floppy hair aside. It's a gesture that Eliza doesn't yet realise will become painfully familiar to her as time passes.

"Yes," the throaty laugh again; he seems pleased with this slice of self-awareness.

They find an empty bench, easier now that the summer is over, the leaves are turning, and the afternoons are darkening. Eliza shivers with cold and the residue of the hangover as she watches Jack stride off to buy supplies from one of the up-cycled police box coffee shops on the edge of the park. The metal segs on his brogues click harmoniously with the iron of the trains clanking and clacking into Waverley Station. The wind is whipping up an urban cyclone, swooping and dipping and scooping up fag buts and sweetie wrappers in a squall from the squalor of the pavements.

Tourists straggle between the seasons, rooted to the spot while they point their cameras at the Scot monument, trying to replicate the postcards they could buy and then throw away again. The older couples wear mountain jackets as if that will keep everything at bay; the younger ones wrap themselves in each other before returning to tangle themselves in their desire and hotel sheets.

Jack reappears, balancing a cardboard drinks carrier with hot chocolate and muffins; Eliza shivers through her Friday night jacket, but Jack's on it and, in a showy act of chivalry, peels off his jumper and thrusts it at her.

"Put it on; you're freezing," he says.

She takes it without protest and pulls it over her jacket. It smells wholesome, of damp wool and soap, he's on detachment from his regiment in Windsor, deployed to a Scottish unit for a few months and stationed at The Castle.

P C CUBITT

Fly Catcher

Synopsis
In West Africa, local people toil on the vast plantation of the corporation, Arranoil. Their land has been stolen and the environment degraded by the intensive production of palm oil. Conditions are harsh and the workers are agitating for change.

When an unknown boy is killed by a falling palm, tensions start to rise. No one knew his name or where he came from, or who brought him to work on the plantation. And there are rumours of slavery. Local activists campaign for justice, but some have paid with their lives.

A UK researcher, Karen Hamm, arrives in the country to investigate stolen aid – millions of dollars sent for the Ebola crisis have gone missing. Karen has a personal history in West Africa and a privileged childhood that has compelled her to return and make a difference.

As her investigations develop, unexpected clues draw Karen into the dangerous world of local politics, corrupt corporations, and the struggle of workers on the palm oil plantations.

After the death of her new friend Songola, a local activist, Karen travels to the plantation to investigate Arranoil *for herself. She is determined to find out the truth about the missing aid but discovers a trail of corruption, slavery and treachery, that leads all the way back to her own government.*

Soon the corporation is on her tail. Powerful interests are at stake and people will stop at nothing to keep her quiet. Caught in a trap, Karen's only refuge is with an adversary, Dorothy, who lives in the shanty town and has ambitions of her own. Together they form an unlikely alliance to get Karen and all her evidence safely out of the country.

Chapter 1: Songola
The black Land Cruiser had been following them ever since they left the lorry park at Bo. It was new and highly polished with blacked-out windows, but no identifiers. No government plates or private registration. No company or agency logo. This was strange – in West Africa, it wasn't customary to hide your wealth.

Fly Catcher

Songola had noticed the cruiser in the motorbike's mirror as they had rounded a bend near the Blama intersection. That was miles back. It was sinister the way it hung behind, passing them several times on the stretch from Bo to Kenema, and then dropping back again. It had parked near the place where they'd stopped to pick up water and phone credit; unknown faces obscured behind the tinted glass. The motorbike would soon be turning off, heading south along the cratered track toward the plantation. What would the cruiser do then: keep following, or stay on the highway?

The cruiser stayed on the highway.

The motorbike taxi made its way bouncing along the track, weaving through a landscape of stumpy bush dotted with banana trees, Songola seated behind the driver. She was a young mother and political activist and was on her way up country to investigate a death on the plantation. The village headman had said conditions on the estate had deteriorated and there'd been an accident involving a child, who had died. The villagers had taken photos of the boy and wanted Songola to go into the plantation with them to see conditions for herself – the dangerous working environment of the palm oil company that employed them. They believed she could help. That she could get justice for the abuse they suffered at the hands of the vast corporation that had stolen their land. *Arranoil*.

Songola felt the weight of their hope.

When she arrived the workers showed her photos of the boy.

The headman explained,

'This boy...maybe his age was seven years.'

'Do you know his village or his name?' she asked.

'Nobody knows,' the headman replied. 'He come every day with the others...many boys...they work together. Their scars...' he drew two fingers across his forehead, '...these tribes are far, far. Maybe he come from Bomba, maybe Kambia.'

Songola feared what this might mean and asked,

'The child was working with many others?'

'That is so,' the headman replied. 'At first...a few. But now we have many boys working. They come from nowhere.'

The boys' tribal scars indicated they were from different regions of the hinterland; unique patterns of scarification etched on their cheekbones or foreheads suggested they were not from those parts. But when the villagers questioned the boys, they were fearful, not even giving their names.

Songola examined the photos. The little boy's frame had been crushed by a falling palm fruit of immense weight and proportions. There were other injuries: spikelet perforations to his skin, old and new lacerations to his legs and feet. The muscles of his arms and shoulders were overly developed for a boy of his age. The child had been worked like a man. And Songola was reminded of her own child, just six months old.

The next day, Songola travelled to the heart of the plantation. There'd been rumours about child slavery, gangs roaming the countryside buying or abducting children, selling them to companies who then forced them to work. But until then people had not wanted to talk, fearful of forces they did not understand. When the child died, the workers brought him back to their village. They did not alert the foreman. They feared a cover-up, that the child's body would simply disappear, and that no one would acknowledge his existence.

When Songola arrived at the harvesting site, the boys were afraid to talk; shy and nervous, perhaps not understanding the Mende language of the southern people. But she cajoled one lad by offering food. He approached shyly, rubbing rough hands against his grimy shorts, munching barefoot among the sharp-edged fronds that littered the plantation floor. He said he was from a remote area of the Eastern Province, close to the Liberian border in the heart of diamond country, and that he had a brother working in a different part of the plantation. Songola suspected his parents had sold them to traffickers who paid a good price for healthy boys.

That night, Songola spent many hours in the hut trying to get a signal on her phone. It was hooked up and charging from a car battery provided by the old woman who owned the hut who rocked to and fro in her chair, her mismatched earrings – one gold hoop, one turquoise drop – glinting as they swayed in the lamplight. Network coverage was weak in this remote area, but Songola persevered, tapping well into the night in the glow of the screen.

At dawn, the motorbike taxi arrived for the return trip to Freetown. Progress was good as they travelled northwest in the early sunshine, warming rays on their backs.

The landscape rolled by like a picture show, groves of raffia palms, dark green mango trees, and banana copses among tall tussocky grasses. The occasional thatched settlement. Everything dry at this time of year, waiting for the rains.

Songola felt the hot metal of the motorbike's engine through the rough denim of her jeans but she felt cool in the breeze, her jacket flapping open, her hands on the grip bar behind. Her driver was well-known to her and trusted, and he leant forward concentrating on the road, the muscles and sinews of his forearms tensing with the vibrations of the rutted track beneath the wheels. Before long they were back on the highway, starting to fill with laden trucks heading for the Liberian border.

Keeping a discreet distance, the black cruiser slipped into position behind. Songola recognised the car from before.

The sun rose higher, its rays growing stronger on her back, her head beginning to sweat under the weight of the helmet, the perspiration lubricating the cushioned interior. Instinctively she moved her hands from the rear grip, wrapping them around the driver whose body tensed, alarmed at the break in cultural norms. But he kept up their speed, clocking up the miles on the dusty highway.

Songola checked the mirror and saw the cruiser had settled into position. It had not made a move to overtake.

A cold dread crept through her body. Her heart rate quickened, beating louder in her chest, adrenalin surging through her veins. As panic took hold her throat constricted. Her T-shirt dampened from the involuntary lactation of her breasts as she thought of her infant child waiting for her return.

The cruiser's engine growled as it sped up, closing the gap. The sun in the mirror blinded Songola momentarily, blocking the vehicle from view. A moment later it was undertaking them, drawing level on the nearside as she and her driver looked across into the blacked-out windows. The sound of scraping metal as the cruiser turned into them, the motorbike driver intuitively swerving to correct their position. Again, the cruiser hit them, this time more violently, and the bike flew wide across the carriageway.

The car had perfectly timed its deadly manoeuvre; the oncoming truck, heavily laden, had no way to avoid them. As the motorbike slewed under the wheels there was an agonising crunch, a tortured scream of metal on metal, and Songola was airborne, bouncing off the cab, flying in slow motion across the dusty shoulder of the road, the sun a burning yellow disc above, the screeching brakes and blare of horns distant as her body reeled and landed on the hard red earth.

Crumpled and still, she lay in the dirt her heart beating violently, loud in her head, demanding attention, thumping the blood through her brain in an instinctive reaction to her body's need.

She felt hands lift her, remove her rucksack, and then carelessly drop her to the ground. Voices fading away. All became still. Far off, unknown birds sang brightly. In the quiet, her breath became slow and gasping, and her heartbeat quietened, slowing. She had no breath or strength, even to feed the fear. She looked up at the sky, so blue, and stared at the small accumulation of cirrus, like fine rippled gauze. A single line of jet contrails lay in the stratosphere, south to north. Helpless. Now she heard no heartbeat, as life ebbed from her, slipping quietly away on the hard-baked earth by the side of the road.

Chapter 2: Lungi
The airbus sank closer to the ground and an irregular patchwork of lamps and braziers emerged from the night to define the contours of activity around the airport. Vehicle headlights could now be seen moving along the bush tracks. Fragmentary illumination in the dense landscape. Then the white runway lights, racing along the ground in their uniform pattern, pointing the way. And the new terminal building with its elegant curved steel roof, smooth and undulating, standing like a beacon in the shadow of the forest.

It was nothing like the concrete shack that I recalled. But that had been thirty years ago and events of great magnitude had occurred since then. Military coups and failed peace accords, the ravages of war and the collapse of the state. Ebola.

But many things remained the same. Like the circumstances of the nation's people, living as they always had with poverty, disease, and bad government. The constant scourge of corrupt politicians.

As I returned to Freetown on that day, I believed I was on a mission to change all that. To discover what had happened to the missing aid. To find out who'd stolen all those millions and to learn how the people felt, governed as they were by greedy pilferers of their state. That day, I was returning to the beloved land of my childhood, believing that I could make a difference.

* * *

A disorderly mass of sweat-drenched passengers clogged immigration while blue-shirted officials roamed amongst them collecting passports, stacking them haphazardly at the booths. Behind the booths stood uniformed personnel, ready to accept a bribe for an escorted shortcut through the terminal. I'd been warned about the tricks at Lungi airport. I hung back, waiting my turn.

Karen Hamm?

I pushed my way to the front, already feeling the heat, my shirt wet under the weight of the rucksack.

The official sat plump in his booth and studied my passport with intent.

'British,' he said, sagely. Without looking up, he held out his hand. 'Immigration card.'

I passed it over and he studied the detail, comparing it to the visa stamp in my passport. There was an uncomfortable pause.

'Business?' he asked.

'Research.' I answered. He peered over wire-framed spectacles that were perched on an enormous nose, his dark skin pockmarked as a passion fruit, his small eyes bloodshot with fatigue.

'I have a letter of introduction,' I said, searching my bag for the university's papers, expecting an interrogation as to my reasons to visit the country. Which were officially, doctoral research. Unofficially, something else.

But the man ignored me, stamping my documents with vigour and shoving them across the desk. He retrieved another passport from the pile and I moved on.

Waiting officials fought amongst themselves to escort me through security. I ignored them. An authoritative type, wearing buttoned epaulettes, signalled with both hands for me to follow but I resisted and stayed in the line lurching its way through to baggage reclaim. The area was packed with bodies: passengers, officials in brown and blue uniforms, masses of street lads working as porters, and ancillary staff, all milling around. The noise was alarming. A strong odour of stale perspiration competed with the Parazone.

Straight away, a number of porters in raggedy clothes descended on me. They shouted in awkward English. One took my arm, another tried to prise the rucksack from my back.

I clung on, panicking.

'Take bag, take bag!' the lad insisted, and I wrestled with him for a while.

This unfathomable style of service was routine, but I knew the notoriety of the country's pickpockets and irrationally concluded that these lads were creating a chance for their mates to do some thieving. The sweat flowed down my face, my shallow confidence disappearing like a drop of rain on the parched African earth.

We moved along; my rucksack with my paperwork, laptop, and all my valuables, was now on the back of a lad in flip-flops, his Man U T-shirt grubby with sweat. Grouped awkwardly, we made our way toward baggage reclaim where bodies stood at the consoles several deep. For each passenger, there were three porters trying to grab a bag and I was shoved to the front to identify mine – a red, hard-shell spinner – being lifted from the other side by a pair of different lads.

'Oi!' I shouted.

A sudden ruckus and one of my porters hurdled the console, grabbed the case and heaved it to our side. Another came up behind, dividing the crowd with his trolley. They secured the red spinner and we moved *en masse* toward customs, the lads clinging like filings to their magnet.

We approached uniformed personnel manning low steel tables and wearing solemn expressions. A short officious woman in a smooth black wig called us to her spot.

'On the table,' she said, in the authoritative manner of petty officialdom.

My entourage positioned the case for inspection.

'Open it,' she said, looking at me hard.

In the secret pocket of my rucksack, which was still on the back of Man U Lad, I found the purse that held the key to the locks on my red suitcase. I handed them over. Security was paramount – I took it very seriously. I knew how difficult it was to replace a lost passport or credit card or anything else in these environs. As I waited, my handlers exchanged meaningful looks with the official. We all waited. Later I was to realise that a bribe had been expected. The woman in the wig sighed and made a superficial rummage through my neatly-folded clothes. Soon everything was zipped up and we were moving swiftly through to arrivals where a young, be-suited man held a card with my name.

'Karen Hamm? Welcome to Freetown, ma.' His smile was broad, his teeth pearly white, his skin the smoothest midnight blue. 'I am Abdou. Sam sent me.'

RUNNER-UP

PAULINE DIAMOND SALIM

I Just Live Here

Synopsis
I Just Live Here *follows three women, Bel, Ina and Elis, as they navigate their separate, interwoven lives following the death of celebrated painter, Duncan Lewis. The parallel narratives follow each woman's efforts to come to terms with the complicated legacy left by the painter, raising questions of whose version of events gets heard and believed.*

Bel is stuck. She's sick of her job as an auctioneer for a snooty Glasgow auction house where she is managing the sale of Duncan Lewis's estate. Her daughter is preparing to leave home to live with her estranged father, against Bel's wishes. Desperate to keep her daughter close, Bel pays her ex-partner off, promising him money in the knowledge that her commission from the auction will soon arrive. But Bel's anxieties around her debt spiral, leading to an outburst that results in her losing her job.

Bel is not the only one under pressure as the auction approaches. Seventy-year-old Ina, who had a decades-long love affair with Duncan, is devastated at being left out of the story being spun around his life, and his reputation as a family man and marriage to another woman.

Downstairs from Duncan's flat, twenty-year-old Elis is living a furtive, unofficial existence, sacked from her job at the local bookies and desperate to keep herself afloat.

The night before the auction, Elis breaks into Duncan Lewis's apartment to see if there is anything of value. There, she bumps into Bel and Ina who have met for the first time. As the hidden connections between the women come to the fore, Bel begins to face up to the choices she has made and glimpses a possible new future for herself, regardless of her daughter's choices. When the day of the auction arrives, it looks very different from what everyone expected.

Bel
There is something illicit about having the keys to a property that's not your own. All summer, Bel had let herself in to the top floor flat at twenty-two Burnside Avenue. She came to know the exact strength needed to

nudge the communal main door open, the mouldering damp laundry smell that rose from the close to the first-floor landing, the wind of the staircase, the still-smooth bottle green late Victorian wall tiles, and the rise and depth of each of the eighty-two steps that led to Duncan Lewis's apartment.

"Not much to see." She turned to Cora, the young journalist, and the bald photographer crowding into the small square hallway behind her. "Kitchen, bathroom," she pointed to the knotted pine doors that opened off the hall. The rooms were stripped, skirting boards scuffed, tea stains on the wall. "And this is where he painted." She led them into the wide front room. Three tall windows lined the far wall, filled with the uppermost leaves and branches of the sycamores growing in the residents' garden below. The bare floorboards beneath the windows were scattered with hard pinpoints of paint and decades of stains and spills and long-dried drips and splashes.

"Let's do it in here," said Cora, bringing her hands together in a single clap.

Bel noticed how young and confident she was, how quick to make decisions. Fine, she thought, let's get this over with. She tugged on her white gloves, tamping the cotton into place between her fingers, and unzipped a large black portfolio.

"What do you think?" She spread a soft cloth on the floor and placed two small canvases on top. Dark oils, midnight blues and blacks, streetscapes of the city below.

"Maybe hold them up against you?" Cora pointed. "In the chair?"

She perched on the leather armchair in the middle of the floor and followed the photographer's instructions to focus on the empty shelves of the bookcase against the far wall.

"You don't need to smile," Cora leaned towards her and whispered.

She felt herself flush and imagined how she must appear to Cora, this young journalist with neat, tanned ankles and shiny hair. Her own navy t-shirt and linen trousers sucked the light and warmth from the August sunshine and drained any colour from her face. She had never known how to dress herself, never figured out what suited her or had any fun with clothes. These days she dressed to project a sense of purpose, to convince herself as much as anyone else that she was a woman who relied on no one, a woman who supported herself and raised her daughter alone, who paid her bills and pension contributions and a donation to a children's charity on the first day of every month. Not a woman who woke at night reeling from dreams of jumping from the high flats just beyond her bedroom window.

"Incredible to think he produced so much work in this place isn't it?" Cora looked around the room, the walls a patchwork of squares and rectangles where paintings once hung. It was a typical top floor Glasgow tenement. Wide bay-windowed front room, back kitchen and two small bedrooms, bare boards and high ceilings and views across the rooftops to the river. "I mean living and painting in these same four rooms for half a century," she shook her head.

"Hard to imagine," Bel placed her hand over a tear in the armchair's leather. When she first began clearing the flat at the start of the summer, the place had felt alive with the painter's energy, still guttering away in the cramped space where he lived and worked for fifty years. Now the rooms were stripped of all his artwork and personal belongings. The few pieces of furniture that remained were worthless; the leather armchair and saggy sofa in the front room, the empty bookcase too large to shift down the four flights of stairs.

"And the all the trauma connected to this place," Cora went on, twisting her mouth as if tasting something rank. "You'd think he'd have moved out after what happened to his wife."

"People just carry on, don't they?" Said Bel. "You just keep going. And then before you know it twenty, forty, fifty years have passed."

Cora frowned. "Do you think he was a monster?"

"I don't think so. I mean I never met him, but I can't imagine – "

"Aren't you interested?" Cora leaned in.

"It's not really my job to be honest." She could smell the coffee from Cora's takeaway cup on the floorboards between them.

"Look up," the photographer barked.

"Sorry," Bel smiled then remembered not to. "I just oversee the auction, you know. It's not my job to get into the personal stuff. What about Baird? Did you get much from him?"

"So-so."

Bel waited. Baird Lewis, the painter's son, had commissioned the sale of his father's estate.

"Quite tight lipped," said Cora.

"He's grieving."

"I get it."

"It'll be bringing up a lot of stuff. And maybe some things just don't fit with his – "

"Version of events?"

"I was going to say memory, of his dad, his family."

"There's always one person isn't there, after a death?" Cora flipped her notebook shut. "One person that gets in there first, sets out their version of the story."

Bel didn't know what to say. This wasn't supposed to be an interview. Why couldn't Cora just write a straight-forward preview of the auction?

Highlight a couple of the works for sale, drop in a short note about Bel being one of only two female Glaswegian auctioneers and send the thing to print?

"It happened in my family," Cora went on. "If you don't challenge it at the start, it settles into fact, you know? This totally partial, one-sided version of who a person was. It becomes The Truth," Cora spread her palms. "And no one in a grieving family dares to challenge The Truth."

"How old are you Cora?"

"Twenty-four. You?"

"Thirty-nine. Tomorrow, actually."

"Oh happy birthday."

Bel grimaced. "Trying not to think about it."

"Okay," Cora stood. "Let's try another one. Over there?"

They moved to the bay window. Bel took off her gloves and chipped at the hard clusters of paint on the window frame. Outside, rows of blonde sandstone tenements sloped down the hill towards the Clyde. In the distance, across the river to the southside, was her own small semi somewhere in the city's outer reaches. She imagined her daughter Caitlin, leaning against the kitchen counter, texting and scrolling and messaging her friends.

"Look at the back wall again please."

She turned and faced the camera. "He had a huge worktable set up here," she said, spreading her arms in the empty space. "You've seen it in the old photos right? Where he used to work. We could hardly shift it. So many years of paint spilled and dripped down the legs. It was practically glued to the floorboards." Cora didn't reply. Bel knew she'd disappointed her by failing to gossip about the painter and his dead wife. But her boss had insisted it was not for discussion. Certain words were to be used – 'loving wife', 'tragic loss'. And others strictly off-limits. She wanted to make it up to Cora though, wracked her mind for any titbits she could offer her, but when she looked up again the photographer was snapping the legs of his tripod shut and Cora was hoisting her tote bag onto her shoulder.

They said goodbye at the front door. The story would run in tomorrow's paper, a last push of publicity before the sale. It was just days away now. Bel felt it galloping toward her, the biggest she'd ever overseen. She put her gloves back on and slid the paintings into sealed wraps of padded plastic, then slotted them into two tight-fitting, foam-lined boxes, exhaling slowly as she clicked the locks into place. Caring for the artworks always settled her, the quiet focus stilling the adrenaline rush of stress that surged through her on a permanent loop these days. She stood up and looked around the flat one last time. Cora had left her empty coffee cup on the floor, her name scrawled in black pen on the cardboard. She swiped it up, then heaved the portfolio onto her shoulder. At the front door, she fished the keys from her pocket and glanced around the hall. Through the half open bedroom door, a flash of emerald caught her eye. She kicked the door wider, left hand holding the case flush against her hip. The room smelled of damp earth, the double bed pushed against the far wall. A green quilt draped off the edge of the bed and trailed on the floorboards. Bel frowned, shifted the weight of the case on her shoulder. The bed had been made up neatly the last time she was here, she was certain. She clutched the keys in one hand and Cora's empty cup in the other. Leave it, she told herself. Cora and the photographer must have disturbed it, scoping out a shot. Sitting on a dead man's bed and letting the blanket fall to the floor.

Ina
She bought every one of the newspapers that mentioned his name. And they all did, it seemed, for weeks after he died. There was a brief period, after the funeral, when his name disappeared from the newspaper pages, but the stories started up once more as the date of the auction approached.

Ina tucked thin white hairs beneath her black beret and felt her head shake a little, the tremor she'd developed since Duncan's death. She wrapped her raincoat around her, the long one he had always thought elegant and somehow French and stepped out into the morning. Down the hill, past the old swimming baths with the skinny ash trees growing out through the roof. Along the high street, the underground rolling beneath the tarmac. She ducked into the newsagent by the gates of the Botanic Gardens, filled Duncan's old duffel bag with armfuls of newspapers, hefted it over her shoulder, winced at the stab in her left trapezius, and heaved it back along the main road and up the stairs to her flat. Inside, she laid each newspaper out on the kitchen table, unfolding and spreading the pages like the sleeves of a freshly laundered shirt.

Duncan Lewis, one of the pillars of modern Scottish painting, has died at the age of 80. Born in Tyneside in 1940 to a cabinetmaker, Lewis moved to Scotland in 1962 to study painting at Glasgow School of Art.

The photo of Duncan spread across the fold. She forced herself to look at it. He stood rigid in paint flecked overalls in the front room at Burnside Avenue. Rooftops and bare branches in the windows behind him. The right angles of black cranes across the river in the dry docks. Twilight falling on the city. It must have been the early seventies. He had just finished the shipyard tryptic and asked Ina to come over to see it. At that point he'd been working on it for a decade, first sketching it out in their early years together, art school undergraduates in the freezing flat. And then, in the years of silence between them, as baby Baird cried out in the cold back bedroom, Duncan had finally completed it. She remembered standing by the door, hardly daring to step inside the room while his wife Marianne was there. The floor was a mess of rags and tall jars of dark ink. His huge oak worktable stood in the middle of the room, dragged out from the window recess. Ina pinned herself against the back wall, Duncan rooted on the other side of the room, framed by the triple bay window, a gash of black paint on his jaw. Marianne stood among the rags between them.

"What do you think?" Duncan's voice was hoarse. He stared at Ina, measuring her reaction.

She kept her eyes on the painting. It was impossible to look at him, here, in this place that had been theirs. This painting that she had known in its first sketches and brushstrokes, its brown and blue paint flecks stuck to the hairs on his forearms as he wrapped them around her in the bedroom across the hall. He was still staring at her, still waiting for her response as the sky darkened in the window behind him. But it was impossible to speak. Impossible to think with the weight of his wife's silence in the room between them. She held her breath. Marianne lifted the camera. None of them spoke. In the photograph Duncan stands rigid, staring off-camera while Ina is absent, entirely out of shot.

He leaves an incomparable legacy, one of the most significant Scottish artists of the 20th century, unforgivably overlooked until so recently.

She could still hear the shutter click. The thud of the front door closing behind her. The drop of the four flights of stairs as she flew from him and Marianne and the dusk falling fast in the top floor flat.

She touched her finger to the photograph in the newspaper spread out on the kitchen table, as if to wipe the smudge of paint from his face. It had been six weeks since the funeral but still these stories kept coming and Marianne's name kept reappearing. His beloved wife. Her tragic early death.

"Enough," Ina announced to the empty kitchen. Beneath the photograph of Duncan, in a small square at the bottom of the page, was a photograph of a woman sitting in his leather armchair in the middle of the empty front room. There was something familiar about the auctioneer's long neck, the concave stoop of her upper body, leaning as if to protect the painting she held in the crook of her arm. Ina straightened her back in the wooden chair and planted her feet on the floor. She had struggled to look at the auction catalogue. A forty-page listing of every piece of work left in Duncan's flat, and more, his books, pamphlets, folk band posters from starry winter nights at the Citizens Bar. All for sale. It was unbearable to look at his life laid out like that, so she had buried it under a pile of cookery books on the highest kitchen shelf. She got up from the table and rifled through the stack, her breath loud in the quiet kitchen. She flicked though the catalogue pages, wrist bones white and narrow. On the back page, a contact number. She pushed her chair away from the table, carted the phone from the hall to the kitchen, dragging its long tacky wire across the checkerboard floor tiles, and set it on the table. It rang once. She clutched it to her ear.

"Good morning. Malarkey's Auctions." The voice down the line was plummy and smug. "How may I help you?"

FIRST PRIZE

LUCY FOSTER

Paradise Beach

Synopsis
Paradise Beach *is the story of Ulises, a fisherman in the town of Santa María on the west coast of Mexico. Narrated from the perspectives of Ulises, his mother Socorro, his wife Lupe, and Teresa, a prostitute in Mexico City, the novel cumulatively recounts the story of this very particular place and one of its most painful tragedies.*

When the novel begins Ulises and his mother are attempting to go on, in the wake of catastrophe. Ulises has grown up in a homemade blue house on the edge of Santa María, with the other fishing families. Full of swagger and lusting after the wealth of the flashy North Americans who visit his coastal paradise, he has been lured into some lucrative side jobs and has become involved in an illicit narco-trafficking circuit that preys on poverty and skilled seamanship at the coastal margins of Mexico, the alternative frontier. When he becomes a father, Ulises tries to detach himself from the unpredictable life he has been leading which angers the cartel for whom he has been working and, as a warning to others, they inflict the worst punishment imaginable. Through flashbacks and fragments we learn that Ulises' son, Kevin, and wife, Lupe, have been kidnapped and taken to the arroyo, *a river in the foothills of the* sierra madre *mountain range, just outside the town. Kevin's body was returned in a box two weeks later, but Lupe has not come back and her body has not been found. Later we meet Teresa, a prostitute who is learning English in Mexico City and it becomes clear that she is also involved in the tragedy. The final part of the novel is narrated by the town itself and explores the effects of the lives of its people on the spirit of a place.*

0
In front of the Hotel Delaluna one wave scrolls in after another. Sun-baked retirees bob in the water like raisins on lilos. A dog sniffs and shits into the sand. Ice cream sky melts from one flavour to the next and the *Sirena IV* tugs around the headland and starts her approach through the shallow water towards the beach. Behind her, attached to a network of chains, yellow

rope and joints of rusty crane from an old shrimper, she drags the whale. Though it is hardly a whale now, this putrid amalgam of incompetence and despair, the festering remnant of wrongs done, emblem of wrongs to come.

Through the binoculars Ulises pans around the bay, back to the boat, the whale, the setting sun behind it opening a glowing portal into the clouds. Melancholy ballads by José José and Juan Gabriel play in the background of his head, their orchestral overtures so rousing at times that his eyes fill with water and he forgets where he is. But he remembers and pans back towards the tourists slathered across the place in swimming costumes. There is a sign wedged into the sand with a message written on fluorescent card in felt-tip pen – PIÑA COLADA 2 FOR 1 ¡Refresh oneself with the Rock'n'roll Drink of the Summer Amigos! – acrylic promises of neon palm trees and striped sun loungers, everything on Paradise Beach is a function of his distaste. A water eel, half-buried in the sand, flaps and rears up suddenly, monstrous, energetic, as a young father pokes at it with a stick and children flinch and squeal. *You foreigners remind me of lettuce.*

The two men on deck are now visible from the beach, inky outlines on the oozing horizon. Cesar, round like a boulder and unsteady on his feet. Pechy, untamed curly hair atop his broom handle body, looks startled even at this distance, a synapsing neuron or a tree in shadow. A black spot sails in an arc over the side of the *Sirena IV* as Cesar throws another empty overboard. The boat lurches forward with a surge of effort from the motor, almost tossing him into its rancid wake. A nod from the shore and Cesar sounds the foghorn and begins to wave his arms wildly at the bathers.

Watching the boat shudder in, three vultures trot along the shoreline like musketeers.

The smell of decomposing whale creeps in on the breeze, attaching itself to every atom of warm evening. A toddler in a pink rubber ring has tottered over to where Ulises stands and watches his angular face as he speaks, uncharacteristically animated, to the space in front of him. *It's been rotting there for days, Pescadora* – lowering the binoculars – *bits of it'll be falling off in the water now, it could actually explode. You see, gases build up, the gases produced in the rotting process, and the body swells from the inside out and the dead flesh gets dryer and weaker, until* – he makes a guttural noise inside his mouth, fingers slowly tracing the line of a mushroom cloud overhead, eyes wide as imaginary whale shrapnel rains over Paradise Beach. The child begins to cry and Ulises nods deferentially to a parent as she is ushered away.

The boat hiccups with greater intensity as the whale reaches the shallows and bumps along the sand. Men, women, children and elderly bathers start to clear the water, holding their noses, some inexplicably shouting – SHARK!

Uneasy in crowds, Ulises retreats further up the beach and takes the joint from behind his ear. There is a lull as the sky dims perceptibly and hotel palm trees are lit up like flares. A speaker starts to play reggaeton music and the gurning Delaluna entertainment staff, in lime green uniforms and matching visors, launch into an ostentatious dance routine to distract the guests from the trawler invading the beach.

The whale is an unearthly silhouette, partially visible above the shallow water, magisterial in the encroaching darkness. It rolls a little and bumps as the waves flap around it, flies lingering about the surface of its enormous bulk. Ulises lets the joint go out, dropping the end into a browning polythene bag of stubs and replacing it in his pocket. He takes out his phone, golden jawline illuminated as he raises it to his ear. *Ready.*

The smell travels like blood seeping through water and pickles the air completely. Margarita smiles turn to acid and every breath the tourists take, damp swimsuits clinging to their bodies, is heavy with putrefying flesh. They begin to think this is not the kind of thing they wanted to see or smell on their holiday. A truck pulls up alongside the hotel and drives a little way onto the sand before unloading eleven men in badgeless uniforms, holding machine guns.

1

Even before the sun had appeared over the top of the *sierra madre*, whose peaks fold like the back and sides of a great armchair around Santa María, first light, hollow and blue, had already arrived in the plaza which was still hung with ragged bunting and sagging balloons from the night before. In the ghostly pre-morning, men and boys swung themselves down from the backs of loaded pick-up trucks, yawning and calling to each other, blowing into steaming cups of thick chocolate-flavoured corn *atole*, ready to rig up for market. Sofía sat on a plastic stool outside her house in the centre of town to watch them, plucking a chicken over a bucket wedged between her legs. When she had finished one, she put the puckered chicken, with a thud, onto the table beside her and set to work on the next. When all ten of the chickens, whose ten necks she had wrung herself, were heaped bald on the table, she put the bucket of blood and gristle specked feathers aside and started to hammer at the chickens with her machete. She struck through bone and sinew, rust-coloured juices sailing off in all directions, until a heap of glistening pink flesh lay on the table. Satisfied, she put the chicken pieces into polythene bags, knotted for sale, brushed the hair from her eyes with a sturdy forearm and wiped her hands on her pinny, covering it with butchery smears.

Across town, in a small blue collage of a house with a new cement floor, Socorro awoke with a start and sat up, breathless, sweat sticking the clothes to her body and the hair to her cheeks. The room smelled of air breathed all night and of hot children, clicking miniature tongues in their tiny throats as they slept. Socorro scrambled over the two boys, Jesús and Heriberto, in the bed beside her – Evelina must have gone next door to Ulises again, *good girl* – and glanced down at her daughter, Minerva, lying on a quilt on the floor. Her head spinning from getting up quickly, Socorro lurched towards the door, one bare foot landing giddily on the cement and then, without warning, the other. Her elder soon, Cesar, was snoring in a stained vest and baseball cap on the sofa. She fired up the table-top stove, mechanically filled the pot with water from the *garrafón* and hauled it over the flame. Then she broke a cinnamon pod over the pot, added the coffee, poured in half a bag of sugar, and shuffled outside to the toilet.

On the road into the centre of town the sun gathered force and speed, heat and light thrumming out through the sky and pounding into the tarmac as Socorro traipsed along it, swaddled in shawls and wheezing heavily, a black veil covering her head. At the bus stop she saw Doña Adela, the statuesque transgender sandwich seller who stood with her basket of thick sandwiches, drinks and *arroz con leche* to sell to the people passing into and out of Santa María. As Socorro came towards her, Adela held out a strong hand which Socorro took and squeezed gratefully, lifting herself to look into the basket *¡mira, que rico nena!* Adela laughed, a deep feminine laugh and took out a plastic cup of sweet thick rice pudding covered in clingfilm and gave it to her, giving Socorro's hand another squeeze as she continued her determined route.

Along the *avenida* buckets of oranges were being slice and squeezed in guillotine-like metal contraptions, juice and fruit flies pouring into plastic cups and polythene bags to be sold with straws. She passed the man with no legs, pulling himself along on his trolley, a piece of plyboard attached directly onto wheels so that he was at ground level, everyone dashing around him to get ready for market. There was a gnarled plastic bowl with a few coins on the plywood plateau next to his stumps, but Socorro kept going, turning back to place the cup of rice pudding onto his plateau with an apologetic nod. She passed the man with curly hair and one extremely long fingernail who sold herbal remedies – a poultice for baldness, tea for the digestion, the kidney function, thyroid activity or anaemia, tinctures for impotence, flatulence and melancholy. He had enormous boxes of dried leaves, one with purple hibiscus leaves for boiling up into *jamaica* water, the next with saffron-coloured leaves, three boxes with shrivelled brown leaves of different shapes, crates of chillies of every size and strength, from crunchy snack to blow-your-brains-out-and-singe-your-vocal-chords hot ones only for the brave.

There was a girl who parked her trailer in the middle of the street, so that Socorro had to hold her breath and apologise profusely to get past her cages of baby chicks dyed fluorescent pink, yellow, green or blue. There were a few fully grown chickens as well, tiptoeing around with residual brightly coloured tufts poking from their backsides. Socorro had given one of these chicks to Evelina on the last market day and the lady had put it in a polythene bag, like a goldfish at a fair, but by the time Evelina arrived home, excitedly clutching her new chick in a bag, all that had been left was an asphyxiated lump of psychedelic feathers. Packed in behind the chickens was the big stall which sold only things made of plastic – wastepaper baskets made of plastic, plastic kitchen implements, ladles, colanders, giant orange spoons, lime squeezers, bowls like the one belonging to the merman on his trolley, baby baths, plastic cribs, clothes pegs, packets containing fifty multi-coloured plastic hairclips, hairbrushes with plastic bristles and airtight plastic pots and boxes.

Socorro passed without pause and made her way out towards the graveyard. The old *panteón* was in the poorest part of town, poorer than the part where she and the other fishing families lived, a part of town where only the dead resided.

To get to the graveyard Socorro had to walk the length of the Calle Pancho Villa which ran parallel to the sea. At the end of Pancho Villa, at the same level as the Hotel Delaluna, was a bridge across the estuary. Over the bridge, stretching as far as the jetty where Our Lady Santa María of the Waters kept her vigil on the perilous volcanic rocks, was a brown wasteland that had once been the place where the jungle met the ocean, the place they now called Gringo Gulch. Here the beachside palms, creepers and broad-footed *higueras* that had stretched across the ground, offering shade down to the sea for the *Huichol* indians on their long pilgrimage from mountain to sacred *aramara*, had been cleared by sun-loving North Americans who built huge white palaces in their place, like boiled sweets unwrapped and tossed into a sandpit. The houses – Casa de Los Amigos, Hacienda Tequila, Villa Vodka – like tiny kingdoms were walled around with bright bougainvillea bushes and hoops of barbed wire, lest local people, lured by the anachronism of opulence, grandeur and shiny surface amid the dust, were tempted to enter in search of the treasures concealed behind their sugar-coated walls. Out in the streets of this rhinestone wasteland, ambivalently positioned snakes of paving leading nowhere, the most presentable and obsequious of the local people stood in the heat of the day with motorised hedge-strimmers and power-hoses, washing four-wheel-drive vehicles amid zealous Spanglish camaraderie with glowing sunburnt employers. Their ice cream makers and satellite television channels, their bread machines and garish water sports equipment.

At the far end of Gringo Gulch, there was a pyramid-shaped house like a Gothic folly built, as if to spite itself, almost entirely without windows. More likely, Socorro thought as she shuffled past, it was built to spite everyone else who would dearly love a window and could never afford to have one put in. In front of the house were electric gates, opening onto its tomblike interior, through which many cars drove with blacked out windows so that no passenger ever had to see the light of day. The only visible window was a porthole close to the pyramid's summit. At this porthole, though Socorro did not see it, was a table, on it a telephone and an ashtray piled high with the half-puffed ends of Cohiba cigars. Beside the table was a straight-backed chair with a view of the street below and the sea beyond.

It was the only house in Gringo Gulch that did not belong to a gringo.

Kevin-Kostner Pantoja López were the words blackened into a wooden cross, staked into the sparse sandy grass of the municipal *panteón*. Beneath the cross was a modest bricked-around rectangle of cement where Socorro knelt and picked up the plastic bottle that served as a vase. There was a label, faded but still stuck to the bottle, which said – LALA Leche Entera – a milk bottle had seemed right, the best she could do, when her daily pilgrimage to this spot had begun eleven months before. Her hand shaking a little, Socorro gripped the wilted orange flowers in the bottle, bunching them by their stalks and tossed them, dripping to one side. They scattered over the next grave along, a princely blue and pink tiled tomb with a garland of multi-coloured plastic flowers wrapped in cellophane, but Socorro never removed her eyes from the grave in front of her. She unwrapped the flowers she had brought, wiry stems picked from the earth-filled petrol cans in which they grew outside her blue house, and put them in the milk bottle, pouring fresh water onto them from a container that she had also carried under her many layers. From the same place she produced a dustpan and brush with which she meticulously swept the concrete, tipping minuscule deposits of dust back into the dust and sand beside her. Hands shaking, she hummed a lullaby as she did this and occasionally stroked the cement's surface, as though smoothing down a blanket over a sleeping body. When she had finished, she rearranged the milk bottle so that its label faced out to the front and, with difficulty, she lifted herself up off her knees and took a step back to examine her work.

HIGHLY COMMENDED

FAIZA HASAN

The Ties that Bind Us

Synopsis

The Ties that Bind Us *is a literary novel examining* **Lina**, **Ollie** *and* **Maya Harding's** *relationship through the lens of trauma. It explores the tensions and guilt arising from illness and motherhood, the push and pull between the rights of one's own body versus the claims of your loved ones. It is also a novel about hunger: for food, for desire and want, for life and then death, for all that life gives and all that it inevitably takes.*

Interspersed with flashbacks of Lina's teenage years as a carer for her dying mother and then her evolution as a famous Michelin star chef, the novel shows her dealing with a fatal, degenerative illness which slowly isolates her from everything and everyone she once held dear. Her marriage falls apart as Ollie struggles with the emotional and financial pressures of looking after a sick partner and running their business.

Knowing that this might be her last chance to mend their challenging relationship, their estranged daughter Maya moves back to care for Lina, hoping that these last few months would help her understand her remote and complicated mother. But as the illness progresses and Lina is forced to give up her kitchen and the life she had so carefully built, she realises that only way she can take back autonomy is to die at Dignitas. Both Ollie and Maya see this as a selfish and cowardly betrayal and questioning Lina's mental and emotional stability, they have her sectioned in a care facility.

Desperate, Lina goes on hunger strike, forcing her family to come to terms with the strength of her desperation and suffering. With no other option but to accept her decision, Maya helps Lina travel to Switzerland, where she takes a lethal injection to end her life.

Chapter 1
Before
Lina

Pain, Lina was fast discovering, came in many different flavours. There was the sudden intense kind – quick, violent, scorching – with the ferocity of a ghost pepper that flooded her mouth with the sharpness of raw garlic and onions. It nearly always took her by surprise and left her desperate for breath, eyes screwed tight, body curled into a ball as she tried frantically to disappear into herself.

Then there was the duller pain that simmered and bubbled under her skin, with a spicy, astringent flavour, as if she'd chewed a mouthful of cardamom or star anise. It was a kind of pervasive, inescapable ache that slowly settled into her very bones until it became part of her body so that hours or days later when it finally disappeared, its loss was its own separate throbbing blow.

This… this was going to be the ghost pepper kind of pain, Lina realised as her mouth flooded with the taste of onions and hot chillies. She swore through gritted teeth, shifting on the hard red plastic chair in the hospital waiting room, bracing herself for impact.

Right on cue her hand spasmed and her fingers involuntarily curled into a tight claw ripping a page from the magazine on her lap, crushing the shiny photographs of happy, healthy people into a tight little ball. A small moan of agony escaped her clenched teeth as short, sharp staccato bursts of electricity raced up and down her arm. She folded over herself, cradling her quivering arm tight against her body, biting down on her lips until she tasted the dull, iron tang of blood.

"It'll pass, it'll pass, it'll pass," she told herself, a litany and a promise she'd been repeating for the past few months to try and keep the fear at bay. And though the pain did eventually pass, the fear had burrowed deep within her as there was a familiar slyness to her symptoms which she'd recognised the very first time her hand had trembled. She had known then, with a certainty that needed no other proof, that her mother's illness – the sum of her inheritance from Maria – had finally woken up and was now poised inside her own body like a coiled, hissing snake.

She inhaled deeply, which turned out to be a mistake. Pain had sharpened her already sensitive chef's nose so that the hospital's harsh metallic odour of disinfectant and medicine combined with the syrupy scent particular to the sick (something akin to rotting fruit) made her gag. With it came sharp flashes of memory tainted with the bitterness of helplessness and heartbreak, of terror and loss and a sorrow so deep that even now after all these years, the mere whiff of it clawed and tore at her. The erratic rasp of her mother's breathing, the touch of Maria's dry, papery hands scraping against her own; her gasps and pleas for release that Lina had been unable and unwilling to grant.

"Lina Harding?"

It took every atom of her being to push the pain away, to shove it and the memories back inside the dark hole where they'd lived for the past forty years and focus on the present. "Here," she rasped. One slow breath in, another out for the count of four. "A minute."

"Are you alright? Do you need help?" asked the receptionist. She placed a hand on Lina's shoulder.

Lina rocked back. At that moment, when it was taking everything to hold herself together, that slight touch was like a hot brand searing her skin.

"Oh. I'm so sorry," the receptionist said, reddening. "I'll get a nurse."

"No." Lina said as firmly as she could. All she needed was a few goddam minutes and the pain would pass. It always did.

In. Out. In. Out. Ignoring the young woman's concern, she focused on clenching and flexing her fingers, willing movement back into the rigid digits, until just as quickly as it had come the pain vanished, and like Pinocchio's wooden hands, hers too came back to life. Their motion was stiff and sluggish though, as if the muscles and tendons were getting their commands from her brain half a beat too late.

Letting out a long shaky exhale, Lina slowly unfolded, one vertebra at a time. She wiped her eyes. "I'm ready now," she said, giving the nurse a tired, shaky smile. It was only then that she realised that people in the waiting room were staring at her with curious pity in their eyes as they recognised her from her numerous television and newspaper appearances. She adjusted her baseball cap and keeping her eyes on the floor shuffled behind the nurse to the neurologist's office.

Mr. Geoffrey Dawson reached across his desk to shake Lina's hand. He was tall, with a large, albatross nose and a charming, warm smile geared towards putting patients at ease. "Sit please," he said, gesturing towards a chair. "A pleasure to meet you. I was at your restaurant just a month ago with my wife for our anniversary. I am something of a foodie, been to many Michelin star restaurants, but your food was like nothing I've ever had before. Unique! Exquisite!"

"Thank you," Lina sank gratefully down into the leather chair.

"Aren't you up for your second Michelin?"

"Third, actually," she corrected absently, using the excuse of settling her bag to gather her breath.

"Third," he repeated, looking suitably impressed. "Isn't that quite a difficult achievement? Not just to earn but to keep three stars."

"It is," she said and left it at that. She looked down pointedly at the open file in front of Dawson.

"Great. Brilliant. So... Tell me," he said, allowing his smile to fade as he folded his arms and slipped from the role of an admirer into that of doctor, "why are you here?"

Lina opened her mouth, stared at him for a moment then closed it. She looked around his office, at the framed certificates, the large window that gave an expansive view of the grey sluggish river, at the large porcelain sculpture of a human brain with all its mysterious pink whorls, searching for something that would help her explain the pain, the loss of control, the fear.

"There's...there's something wrong with me," she said finally.

"Why do you say that?"

"My arm... my right arm, feels funny. Heavy... like rubber. But not all the time. It starts with a tingle, like an electric shock and then I lose all feeling. It hurts. A lot. But then it disappears. My arm... And leg also. I mean... it does come back but... when it all started, I thought it's probably stress or exhaustion. But..."

"But?" Dawson's gaze was steady and encouraging.

Lina shifted in her chair. "It's happening more often now. First my hand and then my foot. I'm never sick. My body is...I have great stamina," she said in a rush. "I'm used to being on my feet and working all day and I exercise and run regularly. But I've been getting so tired... like a drain's opened inside me and emptied everything out. Some days it's a struggle to move and I stumble and trip over my own feet. I have trouble lifting and gripping things. I forget words, orders... I've never done that before."

Dawson nodded as he typed on his computer. "Have you seen any other doctor or physio? Taken anything for the pain?"

"Just my GP. He said there were some abnormalities in my blood tests and referred me to you."

"Yes. I can see those in your file, but we'll need to do more detailed tests. Is there any family history I should be aware of?" When Lina remained quiet, Dawson stopped typing and looked at her. "I know this must be hard," he said gently, his face softening, "but I can only help if I have the full picture. And a family history is an important part of that story."

Lina stared down at her hands. They were well used, dependable hands, with a painter's long fingers, the nails short, unvarnished and cut close to the skin. Her wrists and forearms bore a collection of scars, some recent and pink, others slightly faded, accumulated over the course of her nearly three decades as a chef. She traced the jagged lines of one and thought she felt a whisper of pain.

"My mother. She had it," she said finally. "She was around my age when she developed the first symptom."

She saw Maria, on her white hospital bed, her body still and lifeless while her mind lived on, tubes of different sizes exiting and entering her like a science experiment gone wrong, mummy-like with parchment skin, hollow cheeks and dark feverish eyes. The eyes of a trapped animal.

"Ok. Let's look at you," Dawson pointed towards the examination bed. He handed her a hospital gown and closed the curtain behind him with a loud rattle.

Lina changed slowly, folding her clothes neatly from habit, bra tucked between her shirt and trousers and placed them under the pillow. She struggled with the complicated ties of the hospital gown until with a frustrated sigh she gave up and just tucked the gown around herself as she sat on the bed. "I'm ready," she said, shivering despite the warmth of the room.

Dawson pushed the curtain back and asked her to lie back. He bent over her, poking and prodding, examining her like a chef checking the freshness of a slab of meat. He was so close that she could see the individual hair sprouting from his nose, feel his hot breath as he inspected her arms and then her legs, pulling and pushing. She shifted to stare over his shoulder and out of the window where she could just about make out the onion dome of St. Paul in the distance playing hide and seek amongst the grey rain clouds.

"My mum started falling," she found herself saying softly, almost to herself. "A lot... She'd get these bruises all over her body that looked like yellow, black and blue pansies. Pretty."

Dawson smiled distractedly to show he was listening. "Can you stand up and touch your toes please?"

"She dropped everything. Broke all our plates."

"Walk to the door and back."

"She couldn't move at all near the end," Lina said as she shuffled to the door. She stumbled on her way back and would have fallen if Dawson hadn't grabbed her arm. "See. Sometimes my leg just gives out under me," she said as he helped her hop back on the bed.

He ran the end of a pencil lightly over her arms and then legs and asked if there were areas of her body where she couldn't feel his touch.

"Yes. There. And there...She.... Mum was on a breathing machine with pipes going into her nose and another one feeding her," Lina continued. "It was horrible. She'd make this loud choking noise...It took her such a long time to die."

"Change back into your clothes please." With another loud clatter,

Dawson closed the curtain behind him, all signs of his early joviality gone now.

"I need some blood tests and an MRI," he said, once Lina was back in the chair. "Radiology has a spot in an hour so you can get it done today." The printer whirred to life, spitting out papers that he signed and handed over to her. "The labs are right across my office. My secretary will take you there and book another appointment to see me soon as the results are in."

Lina looked at her watch and shook her head. "I need to get back to work."

"Lina," Dawson said quietly but firmly. "You need to get the tests done today."

She stared at him, at the grim, unsmiling lines of his face. "You think it's what my mother had." It was a statement rather than a question.

"I can't say. Not until we do all the tests," he said.

Numbly, Lina followed his secretary to the lab where they filled tube after tube with blood the colour of ripe cherries, and then to a set of changing rooms where she was asked to remove anything metallic that might interfere with the MRI.

Lina took off her earrings but hesitated when it came to her wedding ring. It was a plain band with a tiny diamond, tarnished and dented after years of abuse in the kitchen. Ollie had offered to have it upgraded to a larger solitaire once their restaurant Faith had received its first Michelin star, but Lina had refused, for it reminded her of a time when she was pregnant and scared and this ring had bound her to Ollie and a promise that he would always look after her. She pulled it off and rubbed at the pale skin underneath, disliking how naked and vulnerable her finger looked without it.

Holding the thin gown close to her body, Lina followed the nurse into a stark white room where most of the space was taken up by the large hollow tube of the MRI scanner. She lay down on a narrow flat tray, shifting her head on the pillow until she was comfortable. The nurse handed her earplugs and then headphones to wear over them, explaining that the machine could be very loud.

"Try and relax and stay as still as possible," said the nurse. "You might want to close your eyes. Some patients go to sleep."

Sleep was far from Lina's mind as she lay with her arms held close to her sides, panic button clutched tightly in one hand. Like a vampire in its coffin, she thought, swallowing a hysterical giggle.

With all outside sound cut off, Lina could hear her heart thudding in the silence, a rapid staccato that sped up and got louder and louder as the tray moved inside the machine and the room disappeared, replaced by the curving white walls of the tube. It was only then that she remembered that fear too had a flavour: a pungent, rancid taste, like that of rotten meat. She could smell it, taste it, feel its foul gristle and sinew catch between her teeth.

    She swallowed a rising nausea as the machine thrummed to life with a loud knocking sound that changed into deafening clicking and clacking as if it was being torn apart by immense gravitational forces. Lina's breathing become shallow, panicked, as an intense claustrophobia, the kind she had not felt in a long time, gripped her. She was eighteen again and much too old to hide under her mother's bed but doing so anyways, with the mattress almost touching her face. She heard her teenage self singing her mother's favourite song, ABBA's *Dancing Queen*, softly, quietly, while on the other side of the door people whispered and ate slices of chocolate cake that Lina had made the night before, the batter enrichened with salt from her tears.

DAVID HILL

The Sunlit Pool of the Finished Image

Synopsis
Novels about art works traditionally focus on the artist or creator as opposed to the painting itself and tend to reinforce the Western-centric view of white, male artistic genius. In my work the narrator is primarily the artwork itself as opposed to the artist and by changing this viewpoint I hope to explore, in a far more rounded manner, the way 'great' art comes into being.

The novel deals with one of the most notorious paintings ever made, Gustave Courbet's L'Origine du Monde *which shows the realistic and close-up depiction of a woman's vagina. This novel seeks to give this painting a voice from under the male gaze.*

The novel follows the painting from her production, through her 157-year existence up to the present day. It tracks her relationships with her four owners. It is a journey that takes us from revolutionary Paris to Nazi controlled Budapest, to the birth of French psychoanalysis in the 1960s. Through this journey the painting describes how it feels to be sexually objectified by her different owners; an Egyptian gambler, a Jewish painter and a French psychoanalyst.

The act of telling this story using the voices of women who were exploited as models and objects, sheds a new light on how we, as a society, look at images which have hitherto been canonised as unimpeachable. This novel seeks to use a painting's experience of the societies through which it has passed to provide an outside view of humanity at its most traumatic and barbaric.

The Sunlit Pool of the Finished Image
A Work of Art-historical Fiction
Book One. The Painting.
Chapter 1
Gustave Courbet pulled the cover off me with a flourish. There, staring directly at me, stood Constance and Khalil Bey. He had a huge grin on his face and was rubbing his hands furiously. Constance, well, she just looked dryly at me. I will never forget the shock of that first encounter: her face was my face, we were one and the same. Is that how she felt as well? How

many times have I returned to that room, how many hours have I spent meditating on that moment of connection? It was the closest we ever got to each other, and so, in a way, the closest I ever came to knowing myself. I scan it in my mind for something I may have missed, a clue, a flicker: the key. But I can never find it. There was a vacant coldness in her glance, a nothingness. She looked neither surprised nor shocked nor pleased. She just stood there stock still, her eyes were empty. For that brief moment she seemed to be more inanimate than me.

Unlike my hair that was spread out in luscious curls around my head, hers was neatly scraped down from a white centre parting and fastened in a tight bun at the back of her head. My one visible eye looked up as if the eyeball was straining to jump out from its socket. My nostrils were cavernous openings that dominated the picture, my reddened lips were parted and all the muscles on my face and neck were taut, accentuated, protruding, as if the skin (including the rather unseemly double chin) was struggling to hold my skeletal structure in check. Constance's face was nothing like this: it was controlled, tight. Her long nasal bone ran straight through the centre of her face drawing one's gaze to her slightly downcast eyes, not her nasal passage. Her white skin was perfumed and subtle, soft, and powdered. And yet it was the same face! The same but so different. She was ephemeral, I was guttural. My one eye looked up towards the heavens like the Virgin Mary receiving the holy spirit: but instead of sacral perfection, with me it was all dirty, all pleasure and pain, desire and shame. Hers glazed with emotionlessness. This was my face and that was hers. I understood quickly that they were not alike at all. Hers was made by God, mine was a sick shadow filtered through the perverted mind of Gustave Courbet. It was *his* view of her face that I had, not the real thing. It was a failure. I knew then that she would never let me keep it. She would take my face away from me and I would spend the rest of my life searching my memory to get it back, to get her back.

I overheard a conversation many years later about an Amazonian tribe called the Kayapo. They flatly refuse to allow themselves to be photographed. An anthropologist and a medic were discussing it in front of where I was hanging. The medic had just returned from a work trip to Brazil and was telling his friend about his experiences. He was told that *akaron kaba* means to *take one's photo* but also means *to steal one's soul*. I latched on to that idea and have never let it go. What links a person with their picture? I suppose in many ways I am the perfect person to ask about this. I am a painted portrait of Constance, or at least I am part of her portrait. Humans view this as a threat, an abomination, a curse. But as a painting I see it the other way around, does that mean that Constance's

The Sunlit Pool of the Finished Image

soul resides in me somehow? Am I indebted to her or her to me and how does that responsibility settle between us? As an old friend of mine once said; every debt needs paying, every single one. Somehow.

What I remember vividly from the small amount of time that we spent together on that first day was not some kind of spiritual connection but rather the distance between us. The sense of otherness that she represented for me. I had no idea what she was thinking or feeling during the moments when we were together. I was not her; I was not in her or part of her. The things I knew from before my production I have learnt from conversation that I have overheard since, either from humans or other objects. (Yes, humans, we objects do communicate with each other, just not in a pitch that you understand; did you think you were the only ones? How vain!) In those brief moments Constance and I spent together, there was no process of osmosis by which her memories and sensations were transmitted to me, no Constance-data download. There was simply a divergence of two similar images, a balance that shifted first one way and then another, like a river that splits in two.

At the time we met she was carrying thirty-four years of life experience more than I was. I was therefore a representation of an aspect of her, a pale shadow. Now, however, I am more than double the age that she was when she died. How can it be that all my experiences, many more than she ever had, could have no impact on what I am today? Back then I was a new-born baby but now I am over one hundred and fifty years old, and she is dead. Is she not merely a representation of me? What is she now: a few photographs, some official documents (birth certificate etc.), some reviews, a series of letters, a portrait by Jules-Émile Saintin that is today listed as lost, a few poems and a bunch of stories? Does she even have a voice? I needed to hear her voice, I needed to discover her lost story. Would she tell me about her career as a ballerina, her childhood, her hopes and dreams: would anyone care for this forgotten woman but me? This sounds arrogant but is it not the case that the only reason anyone would even listen to her story now is to gain a deeper understanding of me? Is that not what I am searching for as well?

"Well? What did I tell you?" Courbet waved his hand at me as he spoke, "Is it not something, is it not magnificent, eh? You thought *Venus and Psyche* was something. You thought *The Sleepers* was good. But that was just foreplay and the aftermath of the event. This is reality right here. This is the event. The depiction of sex on a canvas. The ecstasy of the present, eh, Khalil, what do you think? You must admit. This is special." Courbet danced around me like I was a maypole. He was exerting himself, his huge waistline bouncing up and down. Khalil looked at him like one would look upon an over-energetic dog. Constance just sighed and crossed the room to stare out of the window, she didn't even glance back at me.

"Excellent Gustave." Khalil said, "Of course, excellent. I must say this exceeds even what I could expect. The flesh tone, the delicacy of the hair, it is so real, so wonderfully, um, well, modern, I guess."

"But the head." Courbet exclaimed, "It is my best ever I think." Constance did not even turn around.

"Yes, um, the head. Really good, but, um actually…So, Gustave, Constance and I have been talking and obviously she is worried about her reputation so…" Courbet shot Constance a glaring look.

"What, what! I don't understand. This is what you asked for. I have painted what you ask. A picture of a woman who has just been fucked. I have captured the very moment the man, us, the viewer, has pulled out. We are part of this painting. All of us. Can't you see? It is a masterpiece. I have called it *L'Origine du Monde,* get it? *The Origin of the World.* It is all there. That is where life comes from, from the vagina. From there and from here," Courbet pointed to my hole and then started tapping both sides of his head with his paint-stained fingers. "From here, Khalil, from me, from my hands. I am the artist. I bring forth the origin of the world. *L'Origine c'est moi!*"

Khalil lowered his eyes sheepishly as Constance grunted, "For crying out loud, Khalil! How much longer do we have to listen to this?"

"What did you say?!" Courbet screamed across the room. "You are just a fucking whore!"

"Ok, Gustave. Ok, Constance. Look, let's calm down." Khalil positioned himself in front of Courbet with his small body blocking the path to Constance. For a moment I imagined him been flattened by the obese painter, "I agree it is a masterpiece, of course it is, Gustave. I didn't say anything else. How could I? It's just…it's just."

"For fuck's sake Khalil get on with it," Constance barked, still with her back to the room. She seemed to be growing physically, dominating the whole space.

"Ok, thank you Constance. You are not helping. Look, Gustave, what I actually asked for was the sex of a woman, of Constance. My lucky charm. And that is what you have done, it's great. However, if you want to be technical about it, I never ordered the head."

"Never ordered the head!!!!"

"No, in fact I didn't. Just to be technical. So, in a way the head is surplus to requirements."

"What are you saying?" Courbet shouted, dumbfounded, "You can't have a portrait without a head!"

"Of course, you can, Gustave, it's a picture. It is simply a question of perspective. I am not asking you to do any more work. You have done more than necessary. In fact, I am happy to pay an extra 10% over the agreed fee. There, I can't be fairer than that. It is just a question of shortening the canvas a little, look," Khalil came right up to me so I could feel his breath, like an executioner, and with his pinkie finger he drew an imaginary horizontal line across the canvas, through the line of my neck, "There, you see. It works perfectly. Just a small reduction in the canvas size and we are all good."

Courbet was turning crimson with rage. Khalil stepped back and busied himself with lighting a Turkish cigarette, so he didn't have to look the artist in the eye. He dropped his box of matches with a curse and bent over to pick them up from the paint splattered floorboards. Constance still had not moved from the window. It wasn't even clear she was breathing. I held my breath as one does before a beheading. The artist looked at the little man bent over in front of him and then back at me, did he see pleading in my one eye? He seemed to be bubbling over, on the verge of explosion.

And then suddenly, like a kettle that has boiled and then starts to subside when taken off the heat he deflated. Khalil lifted himself up and finally lit his cigarette. When Courbet eventually spoke, it was in a low menacing voice.

"No. No. I won't cut it," Khalil opened his mouth to respond but before he had the opportunity to say anything Constance had spun around and answered for him:

"Very well. No matter. Khalil let's pay him and go. I am famished. I am dying for lunch. We can sort this later."

Courbet froze at the realisation of what was happening, he looked back and forth between them and then sighed. Constance had already reached the door and swept out of the room. Khalil settled the fee plus 10% and Courbet arranged to have me sent around to Khalil's luxury apartments in Rue Taitbout that very afternoon. Khalil encouragingly slapped him on the shoulder as he left.

"There you go, that's it, excellent stuff. Good man. A real masterpiece. Great work. Congratulations," He backed out of the room, leaving a trail of empty compliments in his wake as he passed the other canvases, "Oh," he said, "I love that one as well. Nice deer, love a deer. Where is that one headed … the Salon, eh? … I will have to see if I can outbid the Académie for it, eh? Lovely work. Good on you.

Whisper it, but in my opinion, you are greater than Delacroix, there, I don't mind saying it. Better than Ingres too and you know I have dealt with them both. Good on you, good man."

I could hear that Constance was already halfway down the stairs. Courbet glanced at me with a strange tremble in his eye. We both knew that I didn't belong to him anymore, that it was out of his hands. For a massive man, he looked so powerless. Then, with a heavy sigh, he reached for the hammer and a bag of nails. I looked at the crates stacked up in the corner. They looked like coffins to me.

HILARY HUDGINS

Pretzel

Synopsis
Pretzel *is the story of a prodigal daughter's return after twenty-two years away. Pina left her younger sister Stef and their grandma Lina when Pina was seventeen and hasn't been home until she arrives, at the opening of the novel, for Lina's eightieth birthday. A story folded in three – the day Pina returns, the week she left, and the day after she returns –* Pretzel *is a book of loving and loathing, cooking and fighting, and judgment and empathy.*

Part 1 (Yesterday)
Stef and Pina spend the day bickering, but Lina is nothing but happy her favourite granddaughter has finally come home – if only they could still cook together in Lina's old restaurant downstairs. The long day ends on a tough note. Lina's dementia wakes the household in the middle of the night, and Pina discovers her sister's mysterious boyfriend is none other than Brendan.

Part 2 (1995)
Pina goes to her special place and finds it's been discovered by a boy from school called Brendan. As the week wears on, his interest in Pina spreads to little Stef. It's me or Stef, Pina thinks, letting an unwanted kiss happen. It's me or Stef, she thinks later, letting much more happen. They run away together to Ireland, where Brendan was born. Just for the summer, she promises her grandmother. But there are some things you do that are so bad you can never come home again.

Part 3 (Today)
The trio head out for a special day. Later, Pina discovers Stef's hiding some injuries, and she knows from experience, Brendan is to blame. Pina knows what she must do. Lina says she will not forgive her granddaughter if she goes again. Pina leaves anyway. There's only one way she knows Stef will be safe.

There was a bony pole of a boy from my class who cleaned fish down on Ninth. Not that they let him sell much of anything, but I'd see him, skinning and filleting and like that. You know the shop that's on the south side of Washington, right on the corner? It didn't used to be there, but their original location, up the block, that's where he worked. I'd walk by most days, and he might look over real quick-like, but nothing more. But there was this one afternoon when he was standing, same as ever, like a stop sign without its top, but like he was, I don't know how to put it, like he was someone else entirely. I thought maybe he was a little taller, but he was already so tall, I wasn't sure I'd have noticed, but when I looked him all the way up, I suddenly knew what it was. All his worries had fallen off him. You know the type who's always nervous? Well, I mean, usually that was him, all shifty looks, mumbled words. But not that day. It was like he'd brushed all his nerves onto the street and left this whole other person. Stiller, prouder maybe. He looked me right in the eyes and pointed his knife, glistening with all those fish scales, down toward my skirt and said, Between the thighs, magic lies. And then he just stood there, smiling this funny little smile, looking right at me. Most of the boys said worse, so I knew he was being sweet, but you know, I mean, you know, he didn't know anything about magic, honey.

Stef nodded, trying very hard not to think too much about her grandmother's magic. He pointed a knife at you when he said this? That sounds terrifying.

Oh no, sweet girl, he didn't mean anything.

Stef unstrapped the blood pressure sleeve, and her grandmother wriggled her arm away like she'd been shackled. Did you know him? Stef asked, penning the numbers into the small, orange notebook.

Well, I knew who he was, but I didn't know him in that way. I was busy knowing Angelo.

Stef tucked the notebook and Velcro cuff into the drawer of the end table. It always stuck. You mean Giuseppe, right? Grandpa Joe.

I mean who I said. This was before your grandfather. You weren't supposed to have anybody till you were married. It's not like now. In my time, you picked one out, just one, and you could have him on your wedding night, but you better not have him before and certainly nobody else. I wasn't a bad girl, but I'd get up to a little something, because I couldn't help it. I was in love. Angelo was my first. Grandma Lina closed her eyes to today. He changed me from the inside, honey, if you know what I mean.

She let out a chuckle that turned into a cough that didn't take, stuck in the back of her throat till her eyes watered. Stef knew better than to offer water till she put her hand out. Somewhere well past the sheer-curtained, second story window and its view of the now quiet corner of Clymer and Eighth, a shadow started to spread, darkening Center City, their block, their neighbours' laundry, the room. But it didn't necessarily mean a storm, not this time of year. So much for any hope of delayed flights.

Grandma Lina had quieted her cough, but her eyes told a different story. Even still she maintained, as ever, a grace that felt salted, cured, and firmed, despite how things were spoiling inside. For decades, Lina had been the co-owner and sole cook at the small but well-loved neighbourhood restaurant right downstairs. Named for her by her adoring husband, who died not long after it opened, it was a place where everyone felt at home because of Lina. No matter what she cooked or how tired she was, she never looked a mess – never had any airs about her either – but absolutely would not once be caught any less than meticulously and radiantly beautiful. She was smaller than she was when Stef was the small one. They'd grown toward each other over the years. But Lina's peppery eyes, sharp nose, and tireless tongue were still snapping and popping under her well-set hair. It was ever moulded into the familiar helmet, even though the hair itself was no longer dark brown or even grey, and instead, very much as white as the cigarettes she never used to be seen without. Lina opened her palm without turning. Stef placed the pale cup into her hand and watched as her lips found the straw, relief spreading across her forehead.

Thank you, honey.

The boy who threatened you with the knife, Stef asked, he did this when you were with your father?

Who threatened me? Now you know I don't know anything about being threatened. She was looking at her granddaughter like Stef had been the threatening one.

The boy who scaled fish, Stef assured her, smoothing Lina's soft head before redoing the quick bun of her own bushy, brown hair. Who said the thing about where magic lies.

Oh, you know, that was sweet of him. Most of the boys said worse. Magic is a worshipping kind of word, isn't it? Must have thought we were made of something very special, which we are, honey, she said, peering at her granddaughter. Poor thing, though. Nobody was going near a boy who smelled like fish, no. Your boyfriend doesn't smell like fish, does he? she asked, giggling.

Stef shook her head with a smile. Thinking about Brendan's smell made Stef restless for him. She wondered if she had time to go see him before everything started tonight. Didn't you always work the market with your father? she asked. What did he say when the boy talked to you like that?

Of course, of course, we always worked together, but he wasn't with me on my afternoon walks. I spent the break different ways, but I usually started at Termini. Papá said the people at Termini had been so good to his older brother in the war, sending fruitcakes. He always had me go up and get a Sorrentino Cookie.

They had a cookie named for the family?

Well, Papá told me it was because I was so sweet that they made those cookies that look like an "S", special for us. Silly, really, but when I was small, I thought they did. He'd give me a penny for my break and would send me to get a Sorrentino Cookie, and I thought I'd died and headed up to heaven, every single day. When I got older, I'd still get the cookie, but then I'd walk down the other side of Ninth and say hi to a girlfriend who worked over that way. If I was lucky, her brother would let her take a break with me, but I wasn't always getting lucky. Lina laughed. You know I'm not talking about that kind of lucky, even though you're going to tease me about Angelo forever now, aren't you, Pina?

Grandma Lina turned toward Stef, her eyes sparkling, and dropped her smile. Oh lord, I thought you were your sister. I know you don't want to hear about none of this, Stefania. Mi dispiace. Can you get me one of the little hard candies in the parlour? I've got this tickle in my throat that— She clutched the cup and took another long sip.

In the hall, Stef leaned on her crutch to pick up the picture next to the candy bowl, seeing it for the first time in years. She and Pina were in front of an old-fashioned boat from a TV show they'd watched at the time. Her sister had loved the idea of living on a boat. Stef couldn't have been hugging her any tighter if she tried.

You spoil me, honey, Lina said when Stef placed the unwrapped candy to her lips. When does your sister get here anyway? It's been a hundred years if it's been a day, bless her.

It's been twenty-two years. Kind of ridiculous we just started mattering now, Stef said, looking at her watch. She should have already landed. I think she'll be here by eleven if traffic's not too bad, she added, tossing a candy into her own mouth.

Just in time for lunch. Now you run along. I know you're making her something special since we're too broken down to pick her up, Grandma Lina said, tapping the walking stick from her chair to the crutch at Stef's side. We can go back to tuna tomorrow, honey, but go on now, so Pina knows how much we missed her.

* * *

Pretzel

I don't feel shit from this mummified weed, do you? Pina handed back the tired joint. Stef shook her head, inhaling a big breath and letting out a messy cough.

Pina slingshot a pair of underwear at Stef's face. Do you remember when we used to wear these? Stef unfolded them to see the old familiar pair, patterned with the word Wednesday. Was getting dressed so complicated we needed the days of the week on our crotch to remind us what to wear? Pina asked.

Between the thighs, magic lies, Stef said, looking at the colourful letters.

What? Pina shrieked with a huge grin. What did you just say?

Stef's eyes still on the underwear, she wondered if it was their mother who'd needed the days of the week. Laundry reminders, maybe. Or knowing what day it was at all. Between the thighs, magic lies, she repeated, looking up.

Pina hadn't really aged at all. Her long brown hair was pulled neatly into the same tiny bun at the base of her little bird neck, her narrow shoulders curving ever so slightly back, as they always had, like she was trying to show off a chest that was never to be or stand a little above everyone else.

Pina squinted her eyes until they closed, her top lip curling like it was ready to spit. You, she said, the tight-mouthed snicker starting, sputtering, totally lost your virginity to someone who used that line, didn't you?

It's not my line, Stef said, throwing the underwear back at her sister. Someone used it on Grandma.

Pina let out a snort and fell to her side, laughing all over the faded carpet in the room they used to share. Grandpa Joe, you sly dog.

It wasn't him. Stef picked up an old viewfinder and started clicking through the pictures.

Oh, it must have been Angelo. That guy broke her open.

You're disgusting, Pina. It wasn't Angelo. Her sister didn't need to know anything else. This story wasn't hers.

Just over the edge of some pictures of the Liberty Bell, click, Independence Hall, click, Pina was still staring. Why do you know this? she asked. Does Grandma have a diary?

She told me. Click. We talk about everything. Click.

She really must be slipping to have said that to you, Saint Stef.

Stef stopped and thought about the sound it would make if she threw the heavy plastic toy at her sister's mouth. Instead, she tried to stand, but her right crutch hit a wooden duck on wheels, and she started to fall. Pina caught her. Slick as ever, sorella, she said, lifting Stef by the armpits.

She wriggled free of her sister, who smelled like one of the essential oils they used to buy on South Street twenty years ago. Stef kicked the duck with her crutch and placed it better. I have to make a call.

Pina raised her eyebrows. You going to tell me about him?

Stef was awkwardly pushing herself up, but Pina stole her crutches before she could use them.

Silence, Pina said, suggests there's something weird about him. She positioned her seat directly on her sister's crucial supports. Is he, Pina paused, a Mormon who came by to convert you and Grandma, and you just pulled him in by the geeky tie and had him all over his pile of Bibles?

Stef glared and opened her hand to ask for her crutches.

Not a religious embarrassment then, Pina went on. Is he a total right-wing nut job who thinks America is the greatest thing since Wonderbread?

There's nothing wrong with liking our country, Stef said.

Except that liking quickly becomes xenophobic obsession over borders that shouldn't exist.

There are so many things you think you know, but you just sound naive and cynical. Some people feel lucky to be born here, and some even come here to have a chance to live as freely we do.

Freely? I can't roll my eyes hard enough right now. Is my own flesh and blood a nationalist? Glad the propaganda machine worked so well on you. Next you'll be telling me not only are borders real, but they should be reinforced with walls to keep all those Others out.

People need jobs, Stef said, giving up on the crutches for now. But no, I think we should welcome immigrants who are willing to work. People who don't share every single one of your opinions don't all fall into one narrow category.

You're disappointingly dumb, Stef. I always thought naïveté was how you spit game, but clearly you've pretended so long, it's reshaped you.

And you're not grateful for the good you had. You've built a habit of dissatisfaction, and so of course our country isn't good enough for you.

Good enough or great enough? Pina smirked. Local sportball team the only red hat you've got in your closet?

Trump wasn't wrong that —

Holy fuck, holy fuck, holy fuck, Pina said, looking at Stef like she was still the little sister she'd left when they were teenagers.

He wasn't wrong that we needed someone outside of our joke of a two-party system, even if he was using that for his own selfish and stupid games.

Well, I agree with you that our system is really just a singly capitalist one, but I don't want to hear a word about that fucking monster.

You want a fight as much as the other side, Stef said, reaching for her crutches under Pina and giving them a hard yank. Pina didn't budge. Don't you think that most people in our country are feeling abused, lied to, and kept down, and maybe we spend too much time yelling at each other instead looking at the real problems? Think of America like two sisters, and you'll start to see the real hopelessness of the problem.

ANGELA HUNTER

A Scrape of Patience

Synopsis
Some people are meant to love you. That doesn't mean they will.

At 8am Margaret delivers Bill to the care of Cedar View. By midnight she will have murdered him but she doesn't know this yet. All that matters for now is getting rid of this forty-year burden.

Bill has never been safe. No one had protected him from his Mother and there won't be anyone to save him tonight when his wife finally runs out of patience. Bullied in childhood, disdained in marriage and bereaved of the only kindness he had ever known, Bill was sentenced to loneliness a lifetime before dementia sealed every exit to the outside world, leaving only the most malignant memories behind.

Whilst Margaret empties her life of Bill, their daughter Stephanie wanders the streets of London, hiding from another tedious day. Forgotten by her husband and with Tom her only friendship of sorts, there's no one to tell that she's hit a wall; that just the thought of walking into her office, her routine, her daily inconsequence, is too much to bear. Memories will compel her to do the right thing, to try. But that time has expired. There is nothing to save.

The move has been too much for Bill. Everything is dislodged, including his secret. The name Judith means nothing to Margaret when she hears it for the first time but it clearly means something to her husband. She finds out, later, when she whispers to Bill to wake up. She finds out who Judith was, and who Bill has never been.

Beneath the pillow, Bill remembers what to do. He counts. Patiently.

March 28th

Margaret
Shoes inside the fridge. Newspapers hanging from a washing line. Piles of neatly folded cardigans in the bath. She had made an appointment with the doctor, knowing. Within weeks he was in pieces throughout the house and across the years. Now he is here, finally, in a room for one.

The sun isn't interested in the window where Margaret stands listening to him being lowered into the armchair behind her. There are no tasks for her to do whilst he is checked out of her world and into theirs. Less than an hour from now the door will close itself behind her and she will return to a house that is no longer a few degrees out.

The carers leave. She checks they've arranged his labelled clothes correctly. Trousers, jumpers, shirts. Vest, pants, socks. Slippers, pyjamas, dressing gown. He doesn't want to take his coat off. He's going to work shortly. No, his mother is coming to take him home. He'd better take it off, the teacher says he's being silly and it's not at all cold.

She doesn't care if he takes it off or not. It makes no difference.

Bill
He is worried and wishes his Mother would walk faster. He's been trying not to ask any questions but the park is just a few streets away and he'd prefer to know now if he's going to be disappointed when they get there. She'll be annoyed at him for interrupting her walk but he really needs to know. 'Excuse me, Mother,' he says to let her know he's about to speak. 'Will the ducks be there?'

'Of course they will, they live there. Where else would they be?'

This is a difficult question. He doesn't know how far they could walk before getting tired. Or lost. And he can't remember if ducks can fly. He finds a different question rather than a response to this one. 'Will they be awake, Mother?'

'Have you ever seen a sleeping duck?'

His Mother doesn't like giving answers. He is six and he knows this already, that she will never really tell him anything. She doesn't talk to him about things, or teach him things, or help him make things. He does his homework alone in the kitchen before dinner and if any of his answers are wrong when she tests him afterwards he only gets half a plate of food. That's why he has to pay so much attention to the teacher in school and not have fun with the other children. It's not nice eating half a dinner. It makes him sad and hungry when he goes to bed. 'No, Mother, but we've never been to the park so early before. What if they haven't woken up yet?'

'I just said they won't be sleeping, didn't I? And even if they were you could wake them up.'

'How?' His Mother shakes him awake every morning. He's allowed one minute to get out of bed before she gets cross. He can't imagine doing that to the ducks. It would scare them.

'You can shout at them or something, I don't know. Use your imagination.'

'But I don't know their names.'

'Oh, for goodness' sake, William, stop worrying! All these questions are getting on my nerves! We're only going to feed some stupid ducks!'

There will be silence now for a long time until his Mother needs to give him an instruction about something. He must be careful to do everything absolutely right. He can't skip or pull on her arm or run ahead or talk. Talking would be the very worst thing he could do. He'll wait patiently whilst she opens the small sandwich bag. No breadcrumbs can fall around his shoes or she'll threaten to drop his breakfast all over the floor when they get home. He'll need to take just the right amount of time to empty the bag; if he does it too quickly she'll make them leave the park right away, too slow and she will snatch the bag away from him and finish the job herself.

For a moment he closes his eyes and hopes that the park gates will be locked. To be locked out removes the many opportunities for trouble on the other side. If they can't get in, his Mother will be angry at the lazy park keeper and not at him. She'll rant at the huge green bars and he'll be able to breathe properly until she remembers it was his fault for asking to visit the ducks when she'd woken him at five o'clock that morning.

But he knows the gates won't be locked. His wishes have never come true before and they probably never will. The gates will be open and everything will go wrong as soon as he walks through them. He leans his head a little to the right, not enough to attract her attention but enough to see that the gates are definitely open.

Maybe he should try to stop them from even getting to the gates. He could pretend to feel sick. Or trip over and graze his knee and cry a lot. He could say he needs to go to the toilet. He could pull his hand out of hers and run ahead, maybe even run right across the road without waiting for her.

He doesn't have the courage to do any of this. So he just keeps walking.

Margaret
'Hello,' he says hesitantly.

Oh for goodness' sake, she only left the room twenty minutes ago to sign some papers and he's forgotten her again already. It's barely worth reminding him. 'It's Margaret.'

'Hi Margaret.'

She walks to the window and pushes the thick red curtain to one side. 'The rain is back on out there.' The point isn't directed at Bill. She has no interest in trying to make conversation with him. She just thinks aloud now and then to hear herself speaking.

'Is it?' he eventually asks, as though a long distance call has only just delivered Margaret's words.

'Yes,' she sighs.

A Scrape of Patience

'That's a shame. Were you outside?'

'No.'

'Did you get wet?'

'I said I wasn't outside.'

'Oh.' He stares at his hands and then asks, 'so how do you know it's raining?'

She ignores him.

'Were you on the bus?'

Still she says nothing, hoping his mind will drop him off somewhere else and save her from another pointless conversation.

'I like the bus. Most of the time I walk though. Mother says I'll get fat and lazy if I take the bus everywhere. Was she on the bus?'

'Of course she wasn't.'

'Really? You didn't see her? What number were you on?'

'I wasn't on a bus.'

'Does the number eleven go past the launderette?'

'The launderette isn't there anymore.' She immediately regrets answering him. It will only cause problems.

'What do you mean?'

'No, the eleven doesn't go past the launderette.'

'Which way does it go?'

'Past the cemetery.' Why does it matter? He'll never see the inside of a bus again. She glances at him in exasperation and wonders if his eyes seem watery. Is he crying again? 'What's wrong?' she asks impatiently.

He shakes his head and puts up a hand as if to say, 'nothing.'

'What are you crying for?'

He clears his throat. 'Sorry.'

'Why are you crying?' Margaret demands more loudly.

He stares down at the round patterned rug in front of his new bed. 'She's buried in that cemetery.'

'I know,' she says and turns back to the window.

Minutes pass in silence. She hears him blow his nose on his handkerchief. From today she won't need to put up with evidence of him around the house. She won't have to listen to the shuffling of his slippers as he wanders around searching for the toilet. No more revolting catarrh noises first thing in the morning. She won't have to hear him slurping his soup following another demonstration of what to do with a spoon. The TV won't wake her up at four o'clock in the morning. And no more random questions about his bloody mother.

'Did you see my mother in the launderette?'

She shakes her head. Back to that, clearly. 'I wasn't in the launderette.'

'She takes the bus. It's a long way for her with all the washing.'

She leans closer to the window. A puddle is forming beneath the rose bush. She's going to get soaked on the way home.

'Do you know my mother? She knows everybody in the launderette.'

And everybody had certainly known her. Margaret finally decides which bit of the duvet to sit on. There really should be another chair in here for visitors. It's not sanitary for people to have to sit on the bed. Or comfortable. Not that he'll have many visitors.

'Do you live near us?' Margaret doesn't answer so he repeats the question. 'Excuse me, Miss? I was asking if you live near us?'

She nods, still looking out of the window.

'Do you live with your mother?'

'No.'

'Are you married?'

'Technically.'

'What does that....?'

'Yes,' she answers angrily. 'It means I am married.'

'What does your husband do?'

Nothing. Absolutely nothing. 'He's retired.'

'He's retired? Goodness, he must be a lot older than you.'

Twenty-two years to be precise.

'He'll be able to take good care of you if he's older,' Bill decides.

She struggles with this Bill who has lost his place and found his tongue after forty years of silent marriage. It wasn't just the talking that had unnerved her when it started. There was the humming and the whistling, the tapping his fingers to a tune in his head. The smiling when he said good morning. She had dropped a plate the first time he'd laughed at a children's TV show in the other room. Life has seemed a happier place for him since he moved into a different version of it.

'Did you see all those tin men?'

'Which tin men?'

'They were in the streets. Everywhere, millions of them. You must have seen them when you were on the bus, they probably slowed your journey down a bit. If you were late it was because of the tin men.'

Surely there must be medication they can give him for these ridiculous hallucinations? 'Tin men don't exist.'

'I'm telling you, Miss, there were millions of them, marching right along the middle of the road. I think they're coming to take us over.'

'No one is coming to take us over.'

'Is there anything about it in the newspaper?'

'No.'

'Have you got one?'

'What?'

'A newspaper. There's bound to be pictures of them in there.'

He can't cope with newspapers anymore. The functions of everyday objects are a mystery to him. 'No, I don't.'

'Could you go and get one? I'll give you money. I want to show you so you can see them for yourself. Great big ten men, millions of them. They were a very shiny silver colour. I couldn't tell if they were friendly, they didn't have faces like ours.'

'There isn't a shop nearby. I'm sure if there are tin men in our streets you'll hear about it on the news tonight.' When are the carers coming back so she can go home?

'No, it might be too late by then, you need to go and buy a newspaper, I want to show you. Here, I'll give you money.'

She tuts. It will be easier to play along, he'll only get himself into a state and at least it'll get her out of this stuffy little room for five minutes. 'I don't need money.' She picks up her handbag. He won't even realise she's gone. She could leave now and he wouldn't be any the wiser. 'I'll be back shortly.'

'Thank you, you're very kind, but be careful out there. Do you want me to come with you?'

'No.' As if he would do anything to protect her in any situation. He's never been a strong man.

TONY IRVIN

The Chameleon Bush

Synopsis
It's hard to become a doctor; far more so if you're an orphan from a Nairobi slum.

When JUMA, his mother RUTH and his older sister PATIENCE become innocent victims of political violence, Ruth takes them from their Nairobi slum to the Kenya coast, where she finds work in a tourist hotel. Here ALI, a driver at the hotel, charms his way into Ruth's life. When Juma contracts malaria, SUNIL, a local Indian doctor, treats him and this initiates Juma's dream of becoming a doctor.

Tourism slumps and Ruth and Ali lose their jobs. Ali then gets a job as a long-distance lorry driver and contracts AIDS. Returning to the coast, he imprisons Juma and Ruth in his stolen van, leaving Patience behind, and forces Ruth into prostitution to obtain the money he needs for his treatment. Ruth and Juma eventually escape, and Ruth finds work with EMMA, a veterinarian working among the Maasai.

Sunil – newly located to Nairobi – has administrative responsibility for Emma's project and falls in love with her. He also administers a project led by ART, an American doctor, researching AIDS. When Ruth dies, Sunil and Emma place Juma in a Nairobi orphanage where Art is secretly using the boys as 'guinea pigs'. When Sunil learns of this, Art shoots himself. Juma finds the body and, fearing he will be accused of murder, flees back to the Maasai.

Ali, meanwhile, robs some Japanese tourists and, despite the reward offered, continues to elude the police. Having squandered his newfound wealth, he sees a television documentary showing Emma's work among the Maasai, with Juma helping. He drives to Maasailand and captures Juma, but an elephant attacks the van killing Ali. Juma survives; the reward money comes to him and his dream finally becomes attainable.

THE CHAMELEON BUSH
PART I
PAMBAZUKO
(The morning light)

"I have seen the desperation and disorder of the powerless: how it twists the lives of children on the streets of... Nairobi."
(Barack Obama, from: *Dreams from my Father*)

Chapter 1

Children play in stagnant pools beside dead dogs. Rats scurry through cracks in walls. Chickens search garbage for maggots. And goats eat plastic bags.

This is Nyumbani: a place where poverty prevails and resilience prospers; where necessity breeds enterprise, hardship spawns resolve, and humour tries to keep desperation at bay. AIDS is rampant, cholera prowls, and infant mortality is too frequent to merit comment, too alarming to appear on official statistics.

Nyumbani assails the senses. A place of noise: of barking dogs, wailing infants, raucous youths, strident women. A place of haggling, swearing, laughing, crying. Even the flickering candle of life is measured in sound: the panting of lovers, the cries of the newborn, the groans of the dying.

In the dry season, the smell of latrines mingles with the aroma of food on charcoal cooking-stoves. Together, these scents swirl into the air with the dust and the rubbish.

In the rains, dust becomes mud and maggots become flies.

Each morning, Nyumbani wakes with the sun, stirs and comes to life, and the cooks, clerks, cleaners, labourers, maids, mechanics, nurses, teachers, drivers, guards, con-men, prostitutes, loungers and scroungers stream into Nairobi to seek their livelihoods and sustain this flourishing international city.

Schoolgirls, in spotless white blouses and blue tunics, appear out of the squalor like newly-emerging butterflies, and walk to school.

The young and the old stay behind and search the rubbish.

Nairobi's lifeblood flows back in the evening and Nyumbani goes to bed with the sun.

Nyumbani brings out the best in people; it brings out the worst. It is kindness and deceit. It is laughter and misery. It is hope and despair. And it is home – whether the dwelling is a ramshackle hut, an abandoned car, or a cardboard shelter – home to a million Kenyans, one of whom is Ruth.

* * *

The one-roomed hut which Ruth rents from a Nairobi businessman is built of corrugated iron sheets, wooden planks and sun-baked clay. With its leaky roof and lack of amenities, there is little to distinguish it from countless similar huts set in the intimacy of poverty in one of the numerous alleyways which grope their way through Nyumbani. Ruth, though, has transformed the inside by painting the walls, hanging a family photo and pinning up her children's drawings. This is the home she shares with her four-year-old son Juma, her seven-year-old daughter Patience, and her mother Njoki, who moved from her own home in Nyeri to help care for the children after their father died. The whispered verdict at the time – slim – lodged a thorn in Ruth's heart.

Each morning, Ruth joins the Nairobi stream on her way to the hotel where she works as a maid, and Patience, her hair tightly braided, joins the butterflies going to school. Juma, whose sharp eyes are invaluable for threading beads, stays at home to help his grandmother make beadwork for the tourist trade.

Scavenging kites and other birds wheel overhead during the day and look down on Juma and Njoki, and on a garbage mountain teeming with people trying to glean subsistence from the waste of their fellow humans. By night, the birds and people sleep, and the mountain becomes the domain of dogs which roam in packs and thrive on the detritus of human misery.

Tension, though, is building in Nyumbani. The fabric of life is changing, crumbling, unravelling. Even the dogs sense it.

Tonight they run by whimpering.

Chapter 2

Ruth sat up, instantly alert.

Squeezed in the bed beside her, Njoki snored, Patience stirred, Juma woke.

'Mama, what is it?'

'Sh.' She put an arm round his shoulder and drew him close, felt the tension in his body as he clung to her.

Footsteps in the alleyway.

She held her breath.

Muffled voices.

The sounds drew nearer and… continued past the door and carried on. Shouting and screaming. Juma buried his face in her neck. Patience woke and whimpered. Ruth reached out comforting arms to shield her children from the sound of households being torn apart.

The Chameleon Bush

Njoki crept to the door to listen, cockroaches scuttling away from her feet.

The sounds faded but the ensuing silence – anxious, fragile, hesitant – was just as agonising.

Only when the footsteps returned and died away into the night, did Ruth relax.

'Things are getting bad,' muttered Njoki, shuffling back to bed.

Ruth settled the children to sleep but she lay awake. She hoped it wouldn't happen, but deep down she knew it was inevitable; inevitable that the unrest which had been building since the election results were declared would spread to the cauldron of tribal tension which was Nyumbani.

Next morning Ruth went to see what help she could give to those who'd been attacked: some maize meal, a few vegetables; sweets for the children and comfort for the traumatised. For Ruth, there was no difference between Kikuyu and Luo, Kalenjin and Kamba; all were Kenyan whatever their tribal background. But others, who'd lived peaceably together for years, looked warily at neighbours whose political affiliations differed from their own – differences exploited by hothead agitators who fanned the dormant embers of tribe and language into flames of stealing, looting and settling of old scores.

Fear prowled the alleyways and encircled the huts. It seeped through shutters, crept through cracks in walls, slithered beneath locked doors. No one felt safe.

The pounding footsteps returned the next night.

The same routine: Ruth's arms of comfort for Juma and Patience, Njoki listening at the door.

This time the footsteps did not continue on.

Whispering outside the door – the door with its feeble lock and flimsy bolts.

The crack of light filtering through the woodwork was blocked.

Juma whimpered. Ruth shushed him.

The whispering stopped. A rat gnawed at something in the roof. A man snored in the adjacent hut. A child called out nearby.

Njoki put her ear to the door.

Ruth and the children cowered on the bed against the wall.

Juma's sharp nails dug into Ruth's arm.

Someone tried the door handle.

'Go away!' shouted Njoki.

'Where's Olembo?'

'He's not here. Go away!'

More whispering.

'Open the door.'

'There's no Olembo here.'

A dog barked.

'Open the door.'

'Olembo doesn't live—'

A crash against the flimsy woodwork. The lock and bolts flew off. The door burst open hurling Njoki backwards. Her head struck the table. She lay still.

Shadowy figures stormed into the hut, ripped pictures off the wall, ransacked cupboards, smashed chairs, turned over the bed and kicked Njoki. No word spoken; their only sound, ragged breathing. When they failed to find Olembo, these silent raiders departed, leaving Ruth and her children frozen in terror.

And Njoki lying in an ever-widening pool of blood.

Someone from a neighbouring hut shouted for quiet.

* * *

In the morning, Ruth will join the Nairobi stream on her way to the hotel where she works as a maid – but not tomorrow.

In the morning, Patience, her hair tightly braided, will join the butterflies going to school – but not tomorrow.

In the morning, Juma will stay at home to help Njoki make beadwork for the tourist trade – but not tomorrow.

Not tomorrow, because Njoki is dead.

Chapter 3

Juma slept fitfully. Every time he woke, he asked the same question: 'Mama, who is Olembo?'

Every time, her anguished answer was the same: 'I don't know.'

He nestled against her and was conscious of warm tears. 'Don't cry, Mama.' He put his arms round her and drifted in and out of sleep. *Why did those bad people come? Who is Olembo? Why does Bibi lie on the floor? What will we…?*

Juma woke with the sun shining on his face through a crack in the wall. He clambered off the bed and peered through the open doorway. The alley was full of people. Some were *wazungu* – white people – and they were pointing cameras and talking into microphones. He'd seen people with cameras and microphones before when an important man in a suit came and talked to a crowd in Nyumbani. Mama said he was called a politician.

The Chameleon Bush

A *mzungu* lady was talking in a loud voice into a microphone but it was hard to understand what she was saying.

"I'm standing here in Nyumbani, Nairobi's largest shantytown and the scene of some of the worst violence since accusations were made of vote-rigging in Kenya's recent elections."

The *mzungu* man beside her pointed his camera at the huts, at torn posters and at pied crows pecking a dead goat. He then swung his camera round, and there was Mama with Patience huddled against her. And what was that shape on the ground, under the blanket, with feet sticking out?

Juma ran outside. 'Mama, what is it?'

"Viewers at home may find some of the images distressing, as tribalism once again rears its ugly head."

The man turned his camera towards the shape on the ground.

'Is that Bibi?' asked Juma.

Ruth nodded.

'Will she get better?'

'Of course not! She's dead,' snapped Patience, and burst into tears.

Juma wondered whether he should start crying now the camera was pointing at him.

"When politics tears a nation apart, it is the poor who suffer." The *mzungu* lady came towards them.

Juma cowered against his mama.

"I've come to interview Mary – not her real name – who with her children was caught up in last night's violence." She held out the microphone. *"Will you tell us in your own words what happened?"*

The man fiddled with the controls on his camera.

"Can you tell our viewers what it was like to have your home destroyed?"

Juma felt Mama silently sobbing.

"I believe your mother died in the attack on your house." The woman smiled and waited. Then said: 'Cut.'

'Does anyone who was attacked speak English?' shouted the man with the camera.

People shuffled their feet and looked away.

'Damn,' said the *mzungu* lady.

'Fuck,' muttered the cameraman.

'Nothing more we can do here,' said the lady. 'Let's go.' She put a sweet in her mouth, a handkerchief to her nose and scraped her shoe against a stone to remove a dog mess.

Juma stared at the *wazungu* as they walked away with their cameras, their microphones and their dirty shoes. A plastic bag fluttered after them.

Ruth bent down to him. 'We have to go to Nyeri today,' she said.
'Why?'
'Because that is where... where we are taking Bibi.'
'Why?'
Ruth stifled a sob. 'To bury her in her Kikuyu homeland.'
'How will we go to that place?'
'A truck is coming to take us.'
Juma waited all day but the truck didn't come.
In the evening some men carried Bibi back into the hut.

Chapter 4

Juma woke after another restless night and lay peering at the shape on the floor. The shape covered by a blanket; the shape that was his grandmother, his *bibi*.

A rat was sniffing it.

He shouted and the rat ran off.

Ruth sat up and Patience woke beside her.

There was a knock on the door.

Juma scrambled off the bed. 'Go away!'

'Who is it?' called Ruth.

'Everything is arranged,' said a man's voice. 'I got a message to your father in Nyeri.'

She moved the chair aside which kept the door shut, and Juma saw his friend, Kamau, who sold the beadwork he and Bibi made. He was waiting with two other men.

'The truck is ready,' said Kamau. 'Can we take her?'

Ruth nodded.

The men came in, wrapped Bibi in the blanket and carried her to a pick-up truck waiting at the end of the alleyway.

'Come, children,' said Ruth.

Juma wore his faded Batman T-shirt and ragged shorts but no shoes because he didn't have any. He clung to his mama's hand. A number of weeping women followed. Most he recognised as neighbours. Some he didn't know.

The pick-up had a big dent in one door and one of its headlights was broken. There were red ribbons tied to the wing mirrors. The driver was leaning against the cab smoking a cigarette. He tossed it aside as they approached and undid the tailgate. The men laid Bibi on the floor of the pick-up then climbed in and sat on the sides. Some of the women also climbed in and squeezed into the cramped space, followed by two more men.

The women were still crying and the men talked in gruff voices.

The driver closed the tailgate, then led Juma to the cab and lifted him in. Patience and Mama sat beside him. There was a plastic dog with a nodding head on the dashboard.

The driver lit another cigarette, climbed into the cab and started the engine.

The crowd moved back as the pick-up set off. People called out words of sympathy. Some waved. Others wiped away tears.

Juma waved back and tried not to breathe in the driver's smoke because he knew smoke was bad for people. He settled against his mama, watched the nodding dog and fell asleep.

HIGHLY COMMENDED

JENNY JACK

Run As If The Devil Were After You

Synopsis

Run As If The Devil Were After You, *a contemporary literary novel, centres around the disappearance of 16-year-old Anwen Merrick from her family's Yorkshire farm in 1994. Seven years later, Anwen's sister, Gwen, encounters a patient in the London psychiatric hospital where she works. Maria is suffering from delusions – but does she hold the key to what happened to Anwen?*

Maria tells Gwen that the Devil took her sister. Gwen is intrigued, but Maria is transferred to another hospital. As Gwen pursues her, against the advice of her partner, Alex, she recalls events following Anwen's disappearance – her encounters with Declan, who runs the village pub, and Jake, the family's lodger, both of whom fall under suspicion. Just as Gwen tracks Maria down, news of her father's death leads her back to the farm. She discovers her mother and younger sister plan to move away, and must choose between London and her childhood home.

Seventeen years later, Gwen's daughter, Ruby, living a sheltered life with her mother in the farmhouse, believes that a woman is stalking her. Helped by fellow loner, Archie, she investigates. At the same time, she determines to find out the identity of her father. Gwen and Ruby argue, and Ruby runs away, hiding in the unused back rooms of the farmhouse. Gwen makes a gruesome discovery, just as Ruby receives a message from a girl, Trudy, who is lost on the road outside, and in possession of a manuscript written by Gwen's grandmother, Lizzie. The manuscript details Lizzie's involvement in a wartime coven, and contains a message for Anwen, not to repeat her grandmother's mistakes. Gradually, through this encounter, Anwen's story is revealed, her clandestine relationship and the trauma which leads to terrible consequences.

1
GWEN
2001

The woman is picked up by police at Elephant and Castle, wearing a white nightgown. It is after midnight. Gwen pictures her drifting alone through the tunnels around the tube station, past abandoned market stalls.

'She says she is Russian,' pronounces Florence, the nurse in charge, as if the woman has declared herself an alien. Not such an unusual occurrence. 'So, maybe you speak to her, hey Gwen?'

'I don't actually speak Russian.'

Gwen shuts her book, but Florence has turned away, arranging papers on the white desk which runs around three sides of the nursing station. Above her head, with its sleek, roped plaits, rows of ring-binders are lined on two shelves. Red and green, inside they tell of walks to the flyover, the lure of attic beams, fears of family members replaced by imposters. Stories Gwen has pieced together as she carries out observations or accompanies patients to the courtyard for a cigarette.

Through the reinforced glass window which looks on to the day room she can see Darren, in vest and tracksuit trousers, watchful as a sphinx against the wall, headphones shielding his ears. Opposite, bent double in an armchair, Val is muttering, a litany of wrongs she has suffered. In a while, Gwen will make some tea, for them, for herself and Florence, for the Russian woman in white on her way up to the ward. Detained for behaving oddly.

Sometimes, if she misses the train from Denmark Hill, Gwen takes the bus through Camberwell to Elephant and Castle. In the evenings, now that the nights are drawing in, she walks *purposefully,* as Alex has instructed her, through the deserted underpasses. Recently, there was a shooting nearby. *But no one will bother you. They will only target you if you are in a gang. If you are one of them.*

Gwen is not *one of them.* She feels her country-ness on her like a cloak, even after the years in Edinburgh. When she walks to the tube, though, she pretends, her shoes slapping on the pavement. On these walks, she has seen people 'behaving oddly'. How odd do you have to be, to get picked up by police?

Beside her, Florence is attaching papers to a clipboard.

'I will bleep the doctor. Tell her we have an admission.'

She pronounces doctor with the stress on each syllable. Her son is studying medicine, a fact she has shared with Gwen each time they have been on shift together. In turn, Gwen has dutifully described her PhD, distilled into a few sentences for anyone brave or foolish enough to ask.

That this has translated into a belief she can speak Russian makes her feel even more fraudulent. She sets her notepad on top of her book, obscuring the picture, the four doomed daughters of the Tsar, all in white, gazing out with clairvoyant solemnity.

'I'll get the room ready.'

Florence nods.

'She will go into room 8. Next to Andrina. They might get along.'

Andrina is Greek, and on arm's length observations after trying to set fire to a can of deodorant. Gwen can't see any reason why they should get along. Still, she can't help but admire Florence's optimism. It does not take long to make up the bed in the bare room, to scan the floor for dropped coins or paperclips. When she returns, Florence is gone. Through the window, across the foyer, Gwen sees her outside one of the interview rooms, gesticulating as she talks to the escorts who have accompanied the patient from the emergency clinic, her free hand tucked into the diamante-encrusted back pocket of her jeans.

Gwen glances down at the desk in front of her. A thin blue cagoule is crumpled there, a rip in one sleeve. Next to it, a red plastic purse. She picks it up, weighs it in her palm, shunts the cagoule along the desk, but there is nothing else there. She had been shocked, at first, at the number of people who come into the hospital with nothing. Sometimes literally nothing, sometimes a plastic bag packed by their community worker – a lighter, tobacco, a change of clothes.

Florence is unlocking the door of the ward with one of the keys attached to her belt, the escorts turning to leave. Behind Florence, the door to the interview room is open, though Gwen can't see inside. Opening the clasp of the purse, she finds a few coins and a train ticket. Sheffield to St Pancras. Gwen regards the words, mundane, familiar, until she hears the door to the nursing station open. She replaces the ticket, snaps the purse closed.

Florence sits, pulling her clipboard towards her.

'She is settled, but we have no details. She says her name is Maria. And she is wearing a hospital gown. Only a hospital gown and her knickers. In this weather.'

In her mind, Gwen swaps the image of a Victorian hysteric in a heavy brocade nightdress for a dishevelled asylum inmate. She touches the cagoule.

'Is this her coat?'

'Yes. It is not warm though, no?' Florence glances up, dismissive, before returning to her paperwork. 'Gwen, you make her a cup of tea, please. We are waiting for the doctor, she will be ten, fifteen minutes.'

* * *

The lukewarm tea slops over Gwen's fingers as she crosses the foyer. *You don't make the tea too hot,* Florence had instructed on her first shift. *If someone very unwell, he might throw it. If you add sugar, it burns worse.* So far, no-one has thrown their tea at Gwen, although she has watched a girl with a palimpsest of scars along her forearm tip a cup of water over the consultant during ward round, watched him sit calmly as the water dripped from his trouser hems on to the floor.

Gwen hopes the tea does not go completely cold before Maria can drink it. Lately, the temperature outside has fallen, the trees stark, the gutters of their Clapham terrace choked with dropped leaves. She has a thin, black scarf which Alex says is as warm as a cobweb, the cashmere scarf he gave her last Christmas still folded in a drawer. Sometimes, standing in the rattling tube carriage, breathing its scents of dewberry and incense, her mind will drift to the girl with the scars, each a precise, careful ellipse. She will think of the keenness of pain, the release.

She had not expected Maria to be wearing lipstick, yet it is the first thing she notices when the woman turns her head. A deep crimson, of rubies and clotted blood, dark against the paper hospital gown, the magnolia wall behind. Someone has given her a white cellular blanket, and it sits like a cloak around her shoulders, making her almost regal. It is only as she comes closer that Gwen sees how the lipstick moves beyond the lines of Maria's mouth. Her skin has a pallid sheen, and a lopsided beauty spot is painted in what looks like eye pencil on one cheek. Her hair, dark, is slicked by rain to her shoulders, drying strands forming a blurry halo. There is a smell in the room, cloying and sweet. It makes Gwen think of the cows crushing into the barn at milking time, the old lame ones at the back. How her father would lift their legs gently, slough off the foot rot with a piece of rope drawn between their hooves.

'Maria? I'm Gwen. I'm a support worker. I brought you some tea.'

She sits in the chair opposite, slides the tea across the low table between them. Maria regards it with a perplexed expression. There is something haughty in her posture, yet her fingers, crooked through the holes in the blanket, are yellowed with nicotine, the nails cracked and split.

'Are you hungry? Can I get you anything else?'

The tea sits on the table, unacknowledged. At last, Maria's eyes swivel towards Gwen. She gives the faintest of head shakes. White crusts the corners of her lips. Beneath her eyes the skin is fragile, bruised, creating hollows echoed in the dips of her collarbone.

Gwen nudges the cup further across the table.

'You should drink something.' She nods at the hospital gown. 'Have you been poorly? In hospital?'

Maria plucks at the stiff material of the gown, mutters something.

'I'm sorry.' Gwen leans forward. 'I didn't quite hear you.'

The woman's gaze fixes on the table. After a moment, she uncrooks her fingers from the blanket and reaches for the teacup. She takes a clumsy sip, balances the cup on her knee.

'I said, I told them what's going on. I told them I need a pregnancy test, and would they fucking listen?'

Her accent is London, not Russian. Her voice rises and cracks, her head jerking up, so her eyes meet Gwen's and the cup pitches sideways. Automatically, Gwen reaches to steady it, but Maria snatches it back. Tea splashes on to the linoleum. At the look on Maria's face, Gwen feels something leap inside her. She thinks of the consultant when the water hit him. She is the one closest to the door – something else Florence taught her.

Very determinedly, Maria sets the cup down on the table. Gwen sees how hard she must work to keep it steady, the clench of her knuckles, her jaw.

'You think you might be pregnant?' she ventures.

'It's what I just said isn't it? Jesus!'

'Have you taken a test?'

Maria's eyes fix on her, grey as pebbles.

'It was him. The neighbour. He made it happen.' Her hand moves on her abdomen, smoothing the hospital gown over her concave stomach, her eyes coming to rest on Gwen's ID badge.

'I know you. Gwen Merrick. Anwen's sister.'

The sweet pain of breathing the scent on her sister's scarf. The shock of the name spoken unexpectedly by a stranger. On the palm of her hand, the girl with the scars on her arms had a single burn, a perfect circle, its edges charred. Gwen had wondered at the time what had made her choose a different type of pain.

'That's right. Not that it's relevant.'

She keeps her voice stiff, though her legs feel shaky. Maria's gaze seems to turn inwards, her pupils darkening. She strokes her stomach, almost reflectively.

'I told them I want it out. They don't get it. I need it cut out of me.' She glares at Gwen. 'I knew who you were, looking at me with her eyes. You know what happened to her?'

'What do you mean?'

Gwen's voice seems to come from somewhere distant. She sees herself as if from above, in the boxy room of cracked magnolia, facing this woman, who claims she is Russian, who claims she is pregnant, who has some strange belief about her neighbour. Always the neighbours, she has noticed.

'The Devil took her.' Maria bunches the fabric of her gown in her fingers. 'He took the laces from her boots and then he strangled her.'

Gwen scrapes back her chair, half rising at the same time as Maria lifts the hospital gown. Carved into her stomach, a gruesome smile, congealed blood glistening like dark berries, its edges seeping pus.

'She wouldn't listen, neither would they,' Maria says. 'I told them I'd do it myself.'

The sweet, rotten smell catches in Gwen's throat, and she almost gags as she backs towards the doorway.

2
1994

The morning after Anwen disappeared, the newspapers reported that the Devil had walked in Yorkshire. The Devil's cloven hooves left their marks in the freshly fallen snow. Through the branches of the ash tree, which sometimes rapped the bedroom window at night, Gwen could see a solitary trail, as if someone had stippled the landscape with black paint. The tracks led across fields paler than the sky, blurring into fog in the distance, and by the time the radio announced the march of Satan, up walls and over rooftops, through Barnsley, Pontefract, Halifax, by the time they realised that Anwen was missing, the wind, which her father said blew straight from the Urals, had swept snow across the strange footprints, brushing them away.

* * *

The night before: Candlemas Eve. At nine o'clock, the door to the Travellers' swung open, and Anwen stood, blinking, on the threshold. Colt's legs in three-inch soled boots, which made her sway slightly. A thick leather choker dripping garnet beads across her throat. She should have worn her scarf, Gwen thought, in this weather. She pulled hard on the beer tap, so the beer streamed out of the glass over her fingers.

'Steady on, love.' Declan Carthy, brother of the landlord, twisted in his barstool. Gwen felt her cheeks grow warm as Anwen approached the bar, dark lips turned downwards like a petulant vampire. Around them, a sheepish murmuring resumed, as eyes which had lifted towards Anwen stared back into the depths of pint glasses.

Gwen took a deep breath, poured the foamy beer down the sink. Glancing up, she saw Declan's tanned arm laid casually on the bar next to his lighter, a sodden beer mat advertising Theakston Ale. Bleached golden hairs and a split thumbnail, the purplish blood of a bruise beneath. He was rebuilding the ruined house behind the pub, coaxing smooth walls from rubble. Gwen watched him shift so that his body was angled towards Anwen.

'Buy you a drink?'

'She's under-age,' Gwen muttered, and Anwen smiled as if she'd said something funny, a gentle, taunting smile. Gwen noted the brightness of her eyes, the unsteadiness in her fingers as she hooked a pack of Silk Cut from her backpack and laid it on the bar.

'Vodka and tonic.' Anwen held her sister's gaze before stowing her bag under her stool. Turning, Gwen glimpsed her image thrown back at her in the mirror behind the bar. Dull skin. Mousy hair. Colourless.

'And one for your sister,' she heard Declan say. She'd been working since seven, and he'd not offered her a drink until Anwen showed up.

'I'm fine.'

Declan winked at Anwen.

'She's too good, she is.' He turned back to Gwen. 'You need to have more fun.'

His eyes were peat brown, like the earth. Something shifted in Gwen's stomach, and she thumped Anwen's drink down on the bar. How old was he? She guessed not far off thirty. Too old for her. Way too old for Anwen. A Celtic tattoo circled his upper arm, muscles straining against the interlocking design. Ostentatious was the word. Gwen felt pleased to have thought of it. The creases of Declan's hands, even the faint crows' feet edging his eyes seemed inlaid with grime.

'Gwen doesn't know the meaning of fun.'

Anwen sipped her drink, liquid trembling on her lower lip. Close up, Gwen could see the centrepiece of her choker, a circle around a five-pointed star, fake jewels casting shadows against her skin. In that moment, Gwen imagined driving a stake through her sister's heart.

SALLYANNE KHAN

Bem's Dream War is Two Centimetres Dilated

Synopsis
Bem's Dream War *is comedy noir ultra-realism. It is a metaphor for the way we are played by government and big business. Of course, the biggest fattest lie is the cost of energy/climate apocalypse and all the luxury and privilege it pays for. This injustice is the beating heart of the story.*

The novel is made up of Chapters of Gonzo-esque short stories on characters, who each represents a different metric of modern Britain, and imagines the things we could do if we did push back. Each tale sees Bem's dream war becoming gradually more and more dilated until it births a full-blown war of total fantasy.

Bem has lived on the Eden Falls estate all his life. He believes his brain will find a solution to all problems. But with words, he comes to realise, he is actually contributing to the background noise of modern life. The only solution is an uprising.

So Bem and the other residents take the fight directly to those that tell us the lies and those that pay them to do so. And as the establishment cracks down on them, it becomes a fight for the survival of either Bem's thinking or the energy companies and the system it funds. A system we are told we all so desperately need.

There are only a handful of people in charge of things in this country, everything flows through them. The issue for our characters is: Are they prepared to risk their freedom and even their lives against an establishment that is not there to serve them.

Bem's Dream War is Two Centimetres Dilated
"Until your own neck has been stamped on, you will not understand what it is to be, fair yeoman." It is Bem's lush baritone, the pied pipering bard of Ganja Towers, reeling them in. "So, hate them sucking on their Ponzi of lies, raw-dogging the decline of man." He had chosen his spot in the lobby well. The hard, tiled walls give him an echo which makes him sound properly awe-inspiring. "Every day we stray a little closer towards their goal. So if you are happy drifting on lulled alibies of corporate denial, thriving off your blindly generated consent; your descendants will

teach their children at breakfast, the worth of your spartan shame." There's a murmur of agreement. "Greed! and its thinking has us mired in troughs, snorting the lines of loathing we were sold, where plenty is never enough." There is applause. A cheer and a whistle or two.

Bem's dream war had gestated for decades in this dilapidated block on the Eden Falls estate many called home. It was once social housing but now, not so much. Now, it was all business. The first four floors were connected by broad walks. They are the community floors where people are expected to mingle. They are peopled by young families, the elderly and the fat-bushed heavy girls on the first floor that would never take the stairs and always Deliveroo'd, in fact anyone who would struggle if the elevators died. These floors could still be considered social because they fulfilled a social need for those that would not be able to find housing elsewhere; but far more importantly, they also free the local authority of any further obligation to house any others in the homes that were built in their name. Modern social care is opaquely cynical, dishonest and manipulative. Local authorities provide it not because they see it as their paid duty. Don't be soft. Local government is not a service. Housing toothless immigrants that satisfy audits and come with a big bag of cash from central government which they don't get for housing the lazypoor in their own borough, looks good in the news. But that does nothing for community. Community for them, is a field in need of constant ploughing. The more it is churned up; the less compact and solid it is, the more muddled its people become and the more they get to grift from them.

Bem had not so much studied these things, he had seen them first-hand and absorbed them. Everything about modern life worships stupidity over knowledge because there's more to exploit with people that know nothing. They are empty vessels looking to be filled with any story you tell them. So ridding the borough of a sense of community is a big step in making those that remain easier to push around. From one dilapidated block on the cusp of redevelopment, to another new shared ownership scheme which retained the council's property portfolio. These, they could sell *and* collect on rents, while shifting all responsibility for its maintenance, security and insurance onto the tenant, who was now a minimal owner with maximum responsibilities. You would have to be stupid or desperate to fall for it and fortunately for those in charge, there's plenty of both around. Filling those schemes with those least likely to raise an objection is a no brainer and dragging a plough through the local community was done best by first ploughing up social housing.

They would claim that turning the underclass over with immigrants and desperados to see if new life springs forth, can only turn up positives because it can't stay as decrepit as it already is forever. Politics will stand in front of any camera, demonstrate with big hand gestures and bulging veins to demand we notice the good it is doing to lives that didn't know they needed improving. And that's the point. They don't need improving. The working-class folk are more than happy being working-class. It's the middle management gougers above them that can see profit where before it would have been unthinkable.

Amongst the working class of Ganja Towers was Mo the horse, the setter-up of squats. He was tough. He ate not just the apple's fleshy fruit, but the core, the pips and the stalk too. Like a horse. He liked to do it when he met someone new because first impressions last and he liked that first impression to speak of his no-nonsense, salt-of-the-earth approach to life. He lived on the tenth floor, across the hall from Pete. He had known Pete for years and respected his knowledge of property law and how it impacted the modern day to day squatting of residences. Pete used to have a drink problem and like a lot of ex-drinkers, when he chose to change his life, he also chose the path of the hoarder. Some choose religion. They are both distractions from their most urgent need to still be drinking. But after he had stopped, Pete discovered he could never again throw anything away. He made stacks of identical items like used coffee cup caps, or take-out food containers, or clothes ruined and beyond repair. His place was crammed with paths worn into the carpet like an elephant might clear in the bush. You couldn't pass on one, you had to wait until the path was clear like a country road and hope you didn't meet something bigger coming the other way. *Why do ex-drinkers hoard?* he had wondered. Is it because they have got so used to collecting bruises, hangovers and scars as the only reminders of the loud evenings they can't remember; that now as an antidote to the chaos of their former drinking life, they collect things entirely unrelated to drink? As a memento of how things used to be. Was that it? Was it all about memory? Before they had none and now they have them piled high around them like totems of their better life.

Like a lot of educated academic folk, Pete conversed like a ninja. He spat out his words like bullets. Clever property folk at the crossroads of law and thuggery generally kept themselves to themselves, their thoughts were not really for showing off anyway. There are always mind-bending amounts of money behind most developments and that money normally came from untraceable places. Developments are the perfect place for mountains of dodgy cash, managed by a thousand City commissions to go and get buried. The development exists to rehabilitate that money so that it can be recycled amongst respectable company basking amongst the townhouses of a Royal Borough.

In his day, Pete often set up villas for Villionaires on the run from corrupt public ownership scandals. These were normally owned by offshore shell companies designed to keep the owner secret and hidden from murders and taxes. But crime is something as a society, we own collectively. The idea that one part of society is more responsible for crime is wrong. Let's face it the only reason rich crooks come over here to destroy the property market and buy the things the government has no business selling, is because we all let them do it. And the luxuries they put on display in this country of fractured poverty, is a testament to how much we care.

What you get with Britain, is sleaze aping as expensively educated advocacy with good tickets to cultural events and Neo-lib banking happy to burn their own children's future to turn a profit. Mostly the Villionaire's homes were empty all year round, save for some domestic staff housed like gimps to let the builders in for the installation of tat and military grade home security. Pete provides Mo with a list of these. And Mo does the rest. Once he knows which Chepstow wedding cake, glowing like beacons of the moral vacuum of dark money that powered them is owned by a company; it is technically no longer covered by UK squatting law. The trouble is, these places may not be protected by law, but they most certainly are protected by any mercenary happy enough to solve a problem quickly, so Mo has to be careful. He has to go into each property knowing there is going to be a reaction and he needs to be ready for that, whenever it comes.

"Like everything else in this country," went on Bem pointing to the map of the estate rivetted to the side of the elevator shaft. "This has been sold to a rabble of cutters and glorious big lies bubbling into an epoch-defining frenzy, to make their extravagance-buffed notion of self, feel known." He lets that sink in and waits for the echo to subside. "They are the blight of our time. Anything the people might think they have a stake in because it was created in their name – they in fact no longer do. Even government is for sale. They don't serve. There's no honour there. The core business of government is running the rule book to benefit anyone willing to pay. Everything else is just distraction."

The floors above the broad walks of Eden Falls were willing to pay. They had become mostly student housing where the rents rise with the uninterrupted views of the city to such a degree, that the forever game overseas student suckers (because only they would find the alternative commute more expensive) can toy with the bedroom to resident designation to such a degree that a two-bedroom on the top floor (aka penthouse) would now typically accommodate six and a husky; with a couple sleeping on a sofa bed in the kitchen-diner and the dog howling at the moon while they party all night long.

But pleasingly for Bem, Ganja Towers with its exotic, inner-city punk vibe, has made most of these young residents a metric of deviance, sacrificing themselves to the hothouse of self-discovery for a better world their degree had no hope of ever satisfying. Away from home they have become the gays, the troons and all other such mystical saints. "The poster rabble for everything the establishment tells us is wrong," Bem would say, "but is in fact, the new beating heart to a better world. All these tower blockers stand on the slippery lip of a magical ectoplasmic force that pulls against the thick cloy of bias, that sees them shackled by debt before their lives have even begun, and tugs at our cuffs not to be saved; but to pull us into the happy maw of unintended consequence with them."

Aiko was one. She was working hard at holding in the first hit of London Skunk she took nine weeks ago and lived in a maisonette near the top with her boyfriend Pietre. She liked his thick-set, hairy body and was unconcerned by his lack of perfect English because it mirrored her own. The language barrier was their pea-green boat. He was her owl and she his pussycat.

Last Sunday she got so nervous when she found out there was one Lotto winner, that she couldn't summon the courage to check her numbers. And as the days passed into a week, she thought it would be easier to just throw the ticket away without checking because the downer of discovering it was not her would be too great: *'You might have a winner there,'* the corner shop guy had joked when she bought it. And in truth, the ticket had felt heavy in the pocket next to her heart the whole way home. She needed to win badly because although she was expected as an Asian student to be rich, nothing could be further from the truth. She was on a scholarship from her father's company and also had to save the money she earnt delivering food at night over the previous two years to top up her award and pay her living expenses. She had to graduate in the top five of her class too, otherwise there was a sanction, and she would have to work it off when she returned home. She didn't even understand how they calculated the sanction, but she got weekly reminders from the accounts department of her father's company which seemed to suggest it could amount to the entire sum plus interest.

But her English was never good enough to get her near the top of class. So she really did need the Lotto win. Then she could send the money home and stay in London with Pietre forever. Statistically there was no chance the winner would be her, but she reasoned if she didn't check, then the four pounds she had invested in the experience was well spent because the possibility of her being the winner was always possible while she didn't know for sure. That delusion worked for a while, but as the weeks became a month, the more she had to convince herself of the opposite; that she *hadn't* in fact won.

Inevitably, she did throw her ticket away. Then, just as she was about to drop the trash down the chute into the dumpster by the boiler in the sub-basement, she caught a glimpse of her ticket's numbers and checked them through the milky pink plastic of the trash bag; mostly because she now could because it was covered in bin juice and had lost its allure. There was nothing wrong with buying a Lotto ticket unless that was all you were doing to get by. And that was the truth of what she had been doing. If, as she stretched the pink plastic tight up against her stained ticket, she discovered she was a loser now, then that would be easier to accept because she had already thrown the ticket away anyway. She had done the same thing when she secretly tried to give up weed. She would throw it away, then dig it out again the following morning. It was truly pathetic. Pietre had stuck to selling and didn't smoke. But she remained anxious and needed to smoke each day to bed. And then he went home because his mother got ill so there was no one watching what she was up to anymore.

When she got really down and couldn't see a path forward, she considered a suicide pact with the neighbour's cat that she sometimes fed. She knew she didn't have the guts to kill herself or indeed any other soul, so she trained the cat through the medium of food to kill them both. She would put its food in a bowl placed over a hair-trigger switch which would discharge a shot gun into her face the moment the food, which was poisoned, was gone. The two of them stayed inside and trained and experimented; then experimented and trained but it never quite came together. In fact, the training gave her a purpose that she had been lacking before and her mood lifted. The cat got fat and friendlier and she realized just in time that she was probably just about to bungle a murder suicide by killing herself first. And the cat would be discovered by Pietre when he returned, chowing down on the little bits of her that had been sprayed around the room.

HIGHLY COMMENDED, DORSET PRIZE

REBEKAH MIRON

Love, I must go

Summary
A woman decides to leave her marriage and set off into the wilderness beyond her country home.

Synopsis
Love, I must go *is a work of literary fiction set over the course of one night in a rural, isolated cottage. The female protagonist, nameless, lives there with her husband, from whom she has become estranged. The novella is addressed to him, though he's absent for the duration. In the first section, "The first few stars", we learn that the protagonist intends to walk out on her marriage but that she's waiting "until the night is deeper, darker still" so that the life she's leaving might be obscured behind her. As she recalls the origins of her relationship, she recounts the small cruelties she ignored in pursuit of being an ideal partner for her husband. This leads into the second section of the novella, "The whole moon", where we learn the protagonist's husband is engaged in an affair. As she remembers his previous infidelities, she becomes convinced there are more secrets to uncover in their home. Finally, in the third section, "The sky as it whitens", the protagonist leaves the house, accepting there will never be a perfect moment to leave, and she may never fully piece together what has happened. As she wanders across the countryside at dawn, she identifies with the wildflowers breaking through the earth and the winter moths disappearing between sunlight dapples. Gradually, she accepts that the woman she has been will not survive the end of her marriage, for she is already becoming something else.*

Themes
This novella centres around the experience of abandonment and betrayal at the hands of a partner. It explores female grief and rage against a backdrop of wildness, which seeks to illustrate nature taking its course, re-establishing balance.

When you left for work this morning, I forgot to ask you when you'd be home.

It occurred to me that I'd been asking you every day for the past year, knocking on the bathroom door as you brushed your teeth or following you across the bedroom as you gathered your things and packed your briefcase.

I didn't want to ask anymore.

I didn't want to hear that you weren't sure; that you'd keep in touch; that you were having drinks with colleagues; that it was a busy day and you couldn't make any guarantees; that I needed to get off your case; that I should make plans without you; that you were sorry.

I didn't want you to come home anymore.

So after you left, I took your toothbrush and threw it in the bin. I added your balled-up socks from the floor and cried because I wasn't sure which ones were mine and which ones were yours. I threw out your expensive perfume too because you always used it as you were leaving, and I craved the base notes, the musk that would come later on. When I got to your underwear drawer, I realised I couldn't remember the last time we'd seen each other naked and so I took off all my clothes. I pushed out my ribs in the bathroom mirror until the bones whitened like two sets of knuckles under skin, two fists.

It's not the being alone as such, although that's certainly part of it.

It's the slanted sunlight through the windows which fades as I cook dinner: one portion for my plate, one portion for later in the fridge. It's the mellow hours of considering a walk or a phone call, or a few pages of a book without ever committing to anything in particular. It's the dull settling of limbs into bed, the intricate folding of oneself into the sheets, always leaving room for someone else. It's the whole night awake, listening to the stillness with such intensity that even the slightest disturbance, the tick of a radiator or the dark brush of a wing at the window, is enough to unsettle the senses.

It's all this time lost, which I can't account for.

Because that's the thing about waiting, you're not always aware that's what you're doing until your world has narrowed to the width of a corridor. A corridor in which I have long been standing at one end, waiting for you to reappear from the other.

Love, I must go

THE FIRST FEW STARS
1

As the night darkens, I stand in my towel at our front window, my hair damp at the base of my neck. There are starlings above the garden pines, murmurating as they usually do at this hour, and winter moths on the outside of the glass, pale scraps of living tissue which seem barely capable of lifting themselves into the air. I've considered going out to sit on our front porch a few times now, but I have goose pimples on the back of my arms in the absence of warm water from the shower. I should dry myself off properly, really, it wouldn't do to catch a chill on top of everything else, but a soft reluctance has settled in my bones that I know won't carry me anywhere at all.

I've recently taken to washing in the evenings, possibly to feel as though I've achieved something, as though I've used my free time in a somewhat productive way. Everyone has to wash at some point, after all, although I've certainly forgotten that at times in the past. And I suppose, if I'm entirely honest, I've often enjoyed the idea that you might arrive home just as I'm stepping out of the steam, ready to wrap my body in one of those thick, fluffy towels we were gifted for our wedding. Or perhaps, more likely, that you might arrive home much later, after I've fallen asleep, and press your nose against my clean, damp hair spread across the pillow.

It's a small indulgence, and one that I'm aware does little to sustain me. Especially when such thoughts are followed by stifled disappointment as you fail to appear or appear with little interest in how clean I may or may not be. Even to mention them here feels like an admission of how my world has come to orbit yours, or rather, to orbit the absence of yours. As though even something as basic as the washing of my own body can't simply be just that; the washing of my own body.

How pathetic, I think, and my reflection quivers against the dark window. The woman I see there is very thin, and I wish she would eat something. Beyond her, the starlings continue to gather and disperse; the whisper of wings displacing the air as they turn over the horizon. There are so many, and as I watch, the flock separates in a way that brings a soft ache to the base of my stomach.

I've developed a new kind of hunger over these past few months. It isn't a craving for food, although the feeling of urgency is much the same. Sometimes I stand in the kitchen as you move around me, and the small of my back, the crook of my neck, the bend at my elbow, all burn to be met with your touch. I've become an expert at maintaining a close distance, just close enough that I might be available to you, should you wish, but just distant enough that you won't find my presence taxing.

Most mornings, I revolve around you in small circles. You distribute a small squeeze of toothpaste onto your brush, and I recede into the corner of the bathroom so as not to appear in the mirror beside you. When I move behind you to retrieve a towel, your back arches away from my hand, and I pretend not to cringe into the shower curtain. When you walk back into the bedroom to get dressed, I wait just a few moments before joining you, taking my time with the spritzing of perfume against my wrists, delicately dabbing the soft skin behind my ears.

After enough of this, you might return, much like how a bird will come to perch on a garden feeder if you wait perfectly still, if you're perfectly patient. This often involves a gentle shoulder pat as you pass by in the hallway or even, on especially good mornings, a goodbye peck on the mouth before leaving. These kisses are not like the kind we shared before; they are ever so light and quick now, as though meeting my lips with yours is part of the same procedure as collecting your keys and wallet before you leave for work. But I still feel they're indicative of something, don't you think? Some lingering feeling, perhaps, or at least some marital obligation. As you go, I hold myself around the waist and count your steps as they crunch over the gravel towards your car.

I've started to believe my skin has cooled by a few degrees as these interactions have become fewer and far between. You are here so infrequently, and the house is too large and cold for one person alone in the winter. I wander about in jumpers and long socks, draping blankets over my knees, pulling my quilt around my shoulders in the evenings when I need to nip to the kitchen. I hold my hands around the kettle as it boils until the heat becomes too much and my palms are sweating and red. I've even slept in a woollen hat on especially cold nights when our bedroom has grown damp, and I couldn't get warm enough to sleep. Sometimes, when I've pressed my fingertips against my cheek in the dark, there has been such a chill there that I've almost wondered whether it's my own touch at all.

It's a very feminine thing to feel the cold in this way. I imagine some, perhaps you included, might suppose this is because women are smaller and milder in body heat, more temperate. But in fact, the opposite is true. A woman's core body temperature is generally higher than a man's, and where the body is used to that warmth, cold air feels even colder on the skin. It's about nerve sensitivity, the perception of cold, which women feel all the more keenly even where a man might be entirely at ease, oblivious to any discomfort. Except, sometimes, I do wonder whether you might think of me here, alone, shivering through a long night in our countryside home, far from the nearest village, and feel some small sense of satisfaction. It's not that I believe you bear me ill will, exactly; it's just a sensation that has begun to creep over me recently. Just as my nerves are sensitive to temperature, so too am I sensitive to your discontent. Your resentment has been gradual, at times barely imperceptible, but it's felt as elemental to me as the turning season.

As I consider this, I drop my towel, which has begun to feel damp and heavy against my body. There's a silver whistle of wind through the window sash, which sings with the cold along the bones of my neck and shoulders. It doesn't take long before my body tenses and begins to shake, but I concentrate instead on a small cobweb that is fluttering nearby; the legs of some poor insect still stuck there against the threads.

I contemplate whether it might have escaped, perhaps with just a limb or two intact, but I feel this is unlikely. There are long-legged spiders laying eggs in our house, their spiderlings transparent and ghostly when they hatch. I've tried to remove them before, gruesome little creatures, but there is no way to keep the outdoors at bay in old houses like these. Limbs of ivy creep up from the skirting board below the kitchen cabinets, snaking between the pipes beneath the sink, and sometimes if the weather is particularly humid, little umbrella mushrooms sprout up from between the bathroom tiles. I suppose it's all part of the negotiation of living somewhere so rural, so entwined with the landscape. But sometimes in my dreams, I imagine these small invasions becoming more eager, more frequent. Our home is covered with vines, and the roots of a tree push up through the floor like a knuckle before a long finger unfurls, beckoning me out.

I know there will be an hour for leaving tonight. The thought has occupied my mind for long enough, and I've decided there can be no other course of action. It's the uncertainty, more than anything, you must understand. If I stay, I will only spend another night lying awake beneath the sheets, wondering whether you might still lift yourself delicately onto the mattress beside me, careful not to disturb the strings, or whether you'll stay out in the night like the wild things that whimper in the woods.

I can't bear to stay, no, but it doesn't quite feel dark enough to leave just yet. The first few stars are out, shining quietly as they pass behind rain clouds, and the moon has begun casting everything in its soft, silver hue.

I'll just wait a while longer, until the night is deeper, darker still, and our house is consumed by it like some unfathomable place I've never known, never lived in, never hoped for.

I suppose I want to leave as though there is nothing behind me.

I suppose you have wanted that too.

MURUNGU

HuKaMa

Synopsis
Hukama means Brotherhood *in the Shona language of Zimbabwe. The story is set today, in the reality of Harare, Zimbabwe. But it could be any city where young boys and girls are homeless.*

Hukama is an inspirational story of brotherhood, bravery, and love.

We follow the lives of two homeless black boys, Themba and Dumi, a Catholic priest, Father Ignatius, and an old white music teacher, Mrs Olver. And Mujiba – an agent for the government who procures young boys for witchcraft. Rituals where young lives are expendable to offer success to the buyer.

In rising tension, the lives of our characters mesh, interweaving, blending the past with the memories of the present.

We watch Themba and Dumi forced to live on the streets, innocents, with only their friendship to protect them from the hazards of drugs, death, and prostitution.

Fr Ignatius is a middle-aged black priest, defeated in his vocation, looking for renewed meaning. He and the white music teacher, Mrs Olver, share a guilt from their past; they could have saved a life. And now, like history repeating, they find themselves involved with Dumi and Temba who seek solace in the Catholic Church of Harare. It is not only drugs and starvation on the streets; Dumi and Themba are targeted. Young boys are prey for 'muti' – a sacrificial witchcraft for politicians and businessmen. Children are murdered for their success.

Street kids are easy pickings.

Against a backdrop of an African city, the story is tense and gripping. The boys' lives unravel in a fast-paced climax of fear and retribution. All their lives are in danger. And few can be trusted.

Will the boys survive? Most important, will the hope of their friendship survive?

Hukama shares their hope, heartbreak, and their love.

HARARE HERALD – July 2023
High Court judge, Justice Munamato Mutevedzi, has handed down the death penalty to Tafadzwa Shamba and Tapiwa Makore senior for the brutal killing of Tapiwa Makore junior, a seven-year-old boy. The shocking crime, which sparked widespread outrage, involved the mutilation and dismemberment of the boy's body for ritual purposes. Shamba, the primary perpetrator, confessed to the horrific deed, saying he killed the boy to sell his body parts to a witchdoctor for US$1,500 to boost their cabbage business.

HuKaMa
Kandiro enda; Kanjiro dzoka.
Little dish go; little dish come back.
Hukama means 'relationship…brotherhood' in the Shona language of Zimbabwe.

Sometime After and Before

Bulawayo
Zimbabwe
'Smoke billowed over the fence. Black. Clouds folded, feeding on themselves. Not a compost fire in a garden. More like a car tyre burning. Putrid, smothering the temple flowers scorching on the trees. People crossed the road, away from the crackle of wet fat burning, a sickly-sweet smell. A lone car, watching from the shadows, slowly pulled away.'

Harare
Zimbabwe
The day is over. Unsettled. The church echoes. Aware of something, perhaps nothing, he pauses, then wipes the chalice of lip marks where he shared the blood of Jesus. Half-lights off the silver as he cleans; a priest, performing daily duties.

Fr Ignatius sighs.

He places the chalice carefully on the table near the door, a priest filling time, to fill time. Shoulders stooped, too much for a man in his forties, resignation arranging props for the morning.

Memories crowd the dark. Shadows lengthen.

Only one person at mass tonight.

Giving up his life… to be a priest… for one person…

He stretches; windows soaring towards the sun, a tired face masking the beauty of youth, a shadow in coloured shafts. His eyes squint at the glare.

Fr Ignatius knows the church as a place of darkness during the day, a sepulchre of secrets, sometimes hope, at night.

He clicks off his collar, prepares to leave the Catholic Cathedral.

A lone car idles outside the church, hidden by the trees.

Watching and waiting.

Dumi
Harare
Before

It was midnight.

Maybe later.

In the silent Harare Park. He had just arrived.

It was a long journey.

Hitching rides on trucks forging through Zimbabwe to South Africa. Driven by large men who needed little sleep and much sex.

One of them slowed down to a crawl as the driver spotted the large eyes of a small boy waving from the bush for a lift.

Dumi had nowhere to leave.

Nowhere to go.

So, he left his mother lying in the hut. Lying very still.

He had to jump to get into the truck. The man did not help him. They didn't speak at all over the hours. Not even when the driver stopped to piss. He signalled the boy to get out of the truck. Dumi had no need to urinate. He had nothing to eat or drink for a day. Maybe two. The man pointed to his large manhood and waved it, so that the stream of urine danced like a fountain. Dumi laughed. He had never seen this before. He stopped smiling when the man pushed his penis into him.

Had he done something wrong? He should not have giggled at the man waving his urine around. He would never forget the pain. Or why the man had done this to him. He wanted his mother.

After it was over, Dumi pulled up his shorts. The man pushed him back to the truck.

He watched the man through the side of his eyes as he was driving. He must have been very bad for the man to punish him like that. Secretly his hand touched his sore place and there was blood.

Dumi began to shake. What if the man stopped the truck again? What had he done? He did not want to be naughty again. He did not want to have pain again.

The road became wider. More cars and trucks. Streetlights flashed by. Maybe they were in Harare.

The truck slowed down.

His shaking became worse. But he would not cry.

The driver veered into a petrol station. No other cars. Just a sleepy man standing by the pump.

The driver shouted at the man to fill the truck. The driver pointed to the gent's toilet, signalled Dumi should follow.

Dumi opened the truck door.

He jumped down and ran headlong into the night traffic. Horns blared; lights flashed. Curses. He did not care. He had to get away. He waved at a taxi Kombi. It stopped. Dumi could not speak. The conductor pushed him inside.

People were laughing. Going into town for a good time. They did not pay any attention to the little boy curled up on the floor.

Then silence. He must have been asleep.

The Kombi stopped. People stumbled out, laughing, adjusting hair and hats. Dumi stared.

This was Harare.

The conductor whistled at him to get out. Poor street kid, but what can one do? They had to come to the city. There was no food or money in the rural areas.

Dumi crawled into another world.

Jacaranda trees and dry grass.

"Unity Square. Independence Garden" laughed the conductor, whistled for more customers, and drove off towards Robert Mugabe Road.

The streetlights made everything look yellow. Even the trees. He had never seen such a thing. Across the road was a bookshop. A large grey building called the Herald. Even the streetlights were yellow.

He felt cold. He was still shivering. Under a Jacaranda tree, a coca cola red tin shack leaned into the shadows. Plastic bottles and bags scattered around it. Dumi blinked. Was that someone behind a tree? It looked like another boy. He walked towards the trees. He was frightened, he was not used to be alone. He shrank into the shadows and watched. Nothing. There was no boy. He was tired. Water trickled down his cheeks. He wiped them away with his arm. It must be his eyes. He never cried. He wanted the shaking to stop. Please God, stop hurting me.

Mrs Olver
Harare
Finishing the final prayer of the rosary, she kissed the crucifix and pushed herself up from the pew. An old pale woman who attended mass twice a day.

To shorten the time.

Struggling the door open onto the evening street, she did not notice two shadows behind the pillar. Watching.

Mrs Olver headed towards her flat across from the church. Waiting for days to pass, interrupted by memories of a life before. Where the mass was Latin, with white priests and white altar boys. Where she offered her tongue for the communion host from white consecrated hands.

Zimbabwe was called Rhodesia then.

A long time ago.

Different now.

Her mind flitted back and forth. The past, the present, trying to make sense. She ate well, lots of broccoli. It helped memory. But today and tomorrow and yesterday were a blur.

She went to mass each evening. And in the morning.

It got her out of the flat, gave form to her day. Divided what was real and not.

Mass was lonely, though. She was the only one.

This black priest... He was always alone. No priests, no friends that she could see.

Some priests were ... after all, they are human...make mistakes, a hard life, they dedicate their lives to the Lord, not allowed a wife or children.

She prayed for them to be strong. Their calling was holy.

He said mass, left immediately, did not talk, except in confession. And when she confessed, he was not listening. As if he had heard her sins before. Was he up to something? besides being a priest? Was she repeating herself? Apostoli ministers and prophets were rich. Their church was just a business. Did this priest have a business on the side?

But you never know in Zimbabwe.

What did her memory want to remember...?

Like her knitting, when she forgot where she was, could not follow the pattern. Unravelled thoughts. She tried to push them away. What was real? Her memories or now?

Her past was Bulawayo. Home for so many years. Teaching music. Running the choir at Our Lady of Lourdes Church. She loved the kids. Such innocent faith. And that young boy Joseph, with a lovely voice.

She hoped Joseph would join the church. She gave him free singing lessons, while his plump white friend waited on her veranda. Seamus. That was his name.

She shuddered. Seamus, a white boy murdered near her home in Bulawayo. They said they killed him for muti, parts of his body cut off, used for witchcraft. Found on a burning compost heap. Only one house down. Near the frangipani trees. Just parts of his body.

This brutal memory would never leave her alone.

People said there was more to his murder, that there was politics involved. That the black men who wanted to get rid of the white leaders had something to do with it. They thought witchcraft would help them She did not know, but she wondered if the boy was a signal, that whites were doomed in Rhodesia.

Nothing happened about the murder. The police gave up.

Such a waste of a young life.

She bit her lip, prayed for the boy's departed soul, for his parents, who lost their only son. Her hand shook as she reached for the prayer missal. Sometimes it was fine, other times, like tonight when she was tired, the shaking was worse. But the Missal would make her feel better. It had a comfortable feel. Take her mind away from the poor boy who was murdered. Why had God allowed it to happen? If only she had ... if only she had.... what? She did not know the danger to this youngster... maybe she could have prevented the boy's death. She should have saved him. He was sitting on her veranda.

Life changed after that. White people lost trust. If a young white could be killed, who was safe? The blacks were not as innocent as they thought. Not as ignorant. Not so tame-able.

She was nervous. Something was wrong, a bad feeling.

She examined the print of small flowers on her dress. Pale green. Of course flowers weren't green, but they were pretty.

Little green flowers. Not real.

Days sliding in and out of memories. Think about something else...

The sun glinted off the window latch. Brass. Old fashioned they would call it, but she made sure it shone like a mirror. You had to keep standards. She didn't mind if it blinded her. She squinted as she rubbed her glasses on the skirt of her dress. Rimless.

Old fashioned...had she thought that before?

Never mind.

So much had happened in her life.

It was Rhodesia when she grew up, not Zimbabwe; named after Cecil John Rhodes, who believed whites must educate and develop the blacks. The locals were half naked, didn't wash themselves, couldn't read. Rhodes' plan sounded like a good idea at the time. Civilize them. Some blacks had other ideas. Joshua Nkomo wanted natives to take over the country. And a man called Mugabe. She never trusted him. His face was like the devil. He spoke like a schoolteacher, but his eyes were too dark. Was he behind the murder of the white boy? He was a troublemaker.

He was the reason that Rhodesia went to war, against his terrorists.

She hated war. Young people dying. So, she helped the soldiers by knitting gloves. Not only for white soldiers, but black soldiers as well.

You did what you could.

Mugabe's blacks would win, it had to happen. There were so few whites in the country.

Whether they could run a government, she did not know. Or care.

This was her country, and that was the end of it. She belonged here as much as the blacks. Her mother was the first baby to be born in Fort Salisbury in the 1890's when the settlers hoisted the Union Jack. A British colony. The empire fought the locals, won, and began farming their land. Introducing civilization. Getting rid of witchcraft, getting them to accept our Lord Jesus Christ.

Her father started a small dairy farm on the Matopos Road. Outside Bulawayo, in the south of the country. Matopos – a sacred area for the Matabele – where spirits lived amongst the giant rocks balanced on each other like a miracle.

She only saw dry grass. Cicadas that deafened her. Leopards that stalked their cows. And a witchdoctor in the compound. He was feared by all the labourers. He threw stones into the dust, said he was talking to the spirits, made different voices, and grunted, talking to the ancestors. He told the workers to kill a cow as the ghosts wanted to eat. "He's the one who is hungry!" Her father laughed at the time. Until he found his prize bull dead.

"Why?" she asked.

"They believe this ancestor witchcraft rubbish. Uncivilised."

She watched the sun sink, yellow and then orange, behind the church.

A movement caught her eye…was that a man under the Jacaranda trees…? Near the car?

But then nothing…must be the sun on her glasses.

Dumi and Temba
Harare

The two boys were still, sheltering each other from the single yellow streetlight. Occasional traffic passed the car parked under the trees, but the boys thought they were invisible, melted into the buttress of the church.

The granite blocks of the church were cold as they leaned against them, waiting for the priest to close the sacristy. Dumi stretched his fingers over the wall, wondering how such big stones had been brought to build their church, their home. His fingers touched Temba's hand and he was glad.

They watched the priest through a crack in the door. Every night, after he had finished mass, the same thing, walk around the church, check the choir loft, turn to close the door. Sometimes they thought he knew they were there. Otherwise, why did he leave the Yale on the sacristy door unlocked?

The boys spoke little, if ever, at night. Night was their secret time. A time of discovery and survival. Their safe time.

Every movement, a look, a gesture had meaning, direction, a sign.

The final click of the door, weary footsteps towards the parked car, the shock of headlights, stone-scrabble under tyres – then silence. The priest was gone.

Alone at last. Dumi and Temba held each other close. Warmth.

Dumi was slight, shorter than Temba, a pale oval face catching the light. Large dark eyes. Temba loved that face.

Dumi fingered his St Christopher medal in his pocket.

His mother's. It was her last gift. His good luck.

YOANNA PAK

Wolnam

Synopsis
Wolnam follows the story of two lives: Tae-Hyun, the father; and Minkyung, the daughter. Two years after leaving her family behind in Toronto, Minkyung and Tae-Hyun's stories converge unexpectedly in Seoul, at the funeral of Tae-Hyun's father, after which Tae-Hyun goes missing.

When the Korean War is stalled with a truce, Tae-Hyun leaves his home in the village of Goksung for a job as a car mechanic in Seoul. Here he meets Geum-Ho. It is Geum-Ho's idea to go to Vietnam, to serve with the Americans, to be paid $50 a month, for a year. Not making enough at the garage to support his family, Tae-Hyun follows Geum-Ho to Vietnam.

Minkyung's childhood in Toronto is difficult with a father whose morals are divided into black and white – God's word vs. the rest. With her older sister, Minha, and her younger brother, Minho, she struggles to live as a Korean at home and as a Canadian at school whilst avoiding the constant threat of beatings from their strict father.

Minkyung eventually relocates to Seoul, seeking to escape the oppressive gaze of her father. However, when her grandfather dies, her father is expected in Seoul for the funeral. A strange man from the past sits alone at the wake watching for Tae-Hyun's arrival. From the man, Geum-Ho, Minkyung learns that her father is a Vietnam War veteran. At Minkyung's insistence, Tae-Hyun agrees to meet with Geum-Ho after the funeral but then, does not return.

Geum-Ho convinces Tae-Hyun to join him in Bukhan Mountain. He has a secret to reveal to Tae-Hyun. Overcome by past demons, Tae-Hyun dies.

Wolnam
Seoul: 2010
They have to grind down the bones. They don't burn like the organs, skin and hair. They get left behind, with the tooth enamel. The mourners watch. We watch and listen, behind the little glass window as the grinding begins. The noise hovers for just a moment above your head and then it descends suddenly – oozing into your skin and making its way through your skeleton, working its way out of your teeth, making you bite down

hard, clenching your jaw and fists. This isn't going to happen again. We won't have to do this for Ahba. We're going to find him. It isn't my fault, right? I'm not my father's keeper. He's the one who's always in charge, always telling me how I should act, behave, think, *be*. He didn't have to go if he didn't want to. Why, then, is it so difficult for me to make the call? It's not my fault. Is it? I've pushed him away too many times and now he's never coming back?

* * *

When I left Toronto for Seoul, my father told me to make sure to visit my grandfather as often as I could. Then he gave me a few thousand dollars to give to the uncle that took care of him. My sister, Minha, asked me to call home once in a while and my brother, Minho, warned me against marrying a *Korean* Korean – a man who would use me as a baby machine, cook and cleaning lady. At the end of my first year, I knew I didn't want to go back to Toronto. Life in Seoul was freeing. Half the world away from a father who divided the world into clear categories of black and white, right and wrong, good and evil, I ventured into what used to be restricted areas of social living. Church was no longer an every week thing, God would forgive sex before marriage, and getting drunk on the weekends (and sometimes during the week) was a part of cultural integration in Seoul social life. There was no one around to hold me to the strict moral code that had shackled me growing up. Aside from visiting relatives once in a while, I had no familial responsibilities. My focus was me. I was liberated.

Then my grandfather died.

I was at work when I got the news. He had gone to take a nap and never woke up. I burst into tears and I wasn't quite sure why. We were not close. The last time I saw him was over a month ago. We had sat awkwardly on the peeling laminate floor of his room in my uncle's house, eating fruit and watching Japanese game shows on television. We didn't talk, just chewed our fruit and laughed once in a while at the asinine tasks attempted by willing contestants.

My department head told me to leave, even though I had one more class to teach, and to take the next few days off. A bereavement was an automatic three days paid leave. Co-workers came to offer their condolences as I shut down my computer and packed my bag. Bowing my head as a goodbye, I left the English Department and hurried out. It was only September, but the trees in the schoolyard were already a glaring yellow. I sat on a bench and called my brother. It was nearly 4:00 a.m. in

Toronto. My father always turned off the ringer before going to bed. Minho would have to drive over from his, 15 minutes away, to tell a man he hardly considered his own father that *his* father had died. With some coercion, Minho agreed to go. My father was told and arrangements were made. Everything was settled.

* * *

Now my father is missing. It's been less than two weeks since my grandfather's death, but here is another departure. I need to call home and let them know. Was it me? Did I make him leave? I am sitting on the roof of my building in Seoul about to make another middle of the night phone call to Toronto, but my ears are filled with the noise of grinding bones.

* * *

Although all of my father's brothers and sisters lived in South Korea, my older sister, Minha, thought that my father should stay with me when he came for Harabuhgee's funeral. I tried to dissuade her over the phone, but she kept asking me how I could even think of saying no. He didn't want to be a burden on any of his younger siblings and couldn't afford to pay for a hotel. And really, how *could* I say no? He *had* to stay with me. I started to count down the days with dread. His presence pushed down on me whenever he shared my space. Neither of us could handle a conversation of small talk. And even now, after thirty years of being his daughter, we couldn't maintain a conversation or keep a comfortable silence.

The day before his arrival, I stood in the middle of my studio apartment. This wasn't going to go well. It was small. Too small. By taking just one step in any direction, I could touch each of the four walls. In a city of nearly 10 million people, it was difficult to find anything larger for a single person. My twin bed was against the wall to my right, under the narrow window. I supposed I should give the bed to my father and sleep on the floor. If I moved the two chairs to either side of the small table, the sleeping mat would just fit. To my left were two hot plates, a mini fridge, microwave and sink – all against the wall separating the living space from the bathroom. He would have to step over me if he needed to use the toilet or get a drink of water at night.

I scanned the photos and gig flyers on the wall above the table, checking to see if there were any that could offend my father's very Christian sensibilities. I left the old black and white Joni Mitchell poster up but took down the flyer advertising a friend's bar that promised two for one Jagerbombs in bold red lettering. Except for one, the candids with friends were okay. None of us looked too drunk. I checked the closet and under the bed for anything that might indicate that I had a boyfriend who sometimes stayed over. I took the condoms out of the nightstand and put them in my bag, to throw away outside.

I needed to change and get to the hospital where my relatives were guarding my grandfather's body. Instead, I sat at the table and thought of the nights out I would miss having my father here. I had moved across the world, was free of his ever-watching gaze, but now we would be under one very small roof. Worse, my boyfriend, who would soon be leaving Seoul to go back to his native England, would not be able to stay over while my father was here. I wouldn't be able to stay at his either. He couldn't exist during my father's stay. He wasn't Korean or Christian. I knew I was being selfish, but I didn't want to share my space with a father who had never really shared himself with me.

* * *

The wailing hit me as soon as I got off the elevators at -3. It was no wonder that the hospital had placed the rooms for funeral wakes far below ground. Patients with even the smallest hope of recovery stayed above. I followed the wailing around two corners before being confronted with a split – sounds of anguish spewed out from four different rooms. I scanned the placards in front of each doorway for my grandfather's name. Carefully sidestepping the white floral arrangements that reached the ceiling, I walked into the second room on the right. It smelled of seaweed soup and kimchi. Groups of mourners sat on the floor at low tables, with heads close together. A few people were scattered about, sipping soju out of shot glasses in solitary contemplation. The wailing drifted out of a doorway to the left of the tables and combined with the smells coming from the kitchen at the back of the room. It hovered over the space like a mournful spirit. One of my cousins was busy distributing Styrofoam bowls half-filled with soup, while another placed small plates of banchan and rice on each table. Their mother, my father's youngest sister, a floral apron wrapped around her white hanbok, made sure empty soju bottles were quickly switched with full ones. She stopped when she saw me.

"Minkyung, you're finally here." She smiled up at me with a flawlessly made up face, framed with dark short curls.

"Yes, Small Goh-Moh," I said, tying my long hair back from my makeup-free face. "What should I do? Do you want me to help you with the tables?"

"Good Minkyung, you can wipe down the tables whenever someone gets up. But first, you need to go pay your respects." She gently pushed me towards the doorway on the left.

    I paused before stepping into the room. My eldest aunt lay face down on the floor, surrounded by the white skirts of her hanbok, under a framed photograph of my grandfather. He hung, serene and wise, on the wall above the closed wooden coffin with black ribbons taped across the two top corners of the frame. The smell of incense was overpowering in the windowless room. My youngest uncle tried to comfort her, but she recoiled at his touch and continued screaming incoherently under the photograph. My eldest uncle stood next to the coffin. Stone-faced, he was absolutely still, staring at nothing. My other aunt and uncle stood next to him, ordered by their ages – the men in black western suits, the women in traditional hanboks. I pulled my black sweater down over my black pants, tightened my ponytail and wished that I had dressed in something more formal. This was my family but I was the foreigner. If only my brother and sister were here.

    The closed room felt unbearably warm and sweat beads formed on my upper lip as I wondered what to do. Thankfully, my youngest uncle came and stood next to me. He gently took my elbow and led me to the coffin. Keeping my head bowed, I moved as close as I could to the photograph, next to my prostrated aunt. My uncle whispered that I should bow three times before he left to return to his position next to the others. I knelt down and brought the backs of my hands to my forehead before bringing my head to the floor. My forehead was hot on my hands as they pressed against the cool laminate flooring. I stood up and did the same twice more. On the third bow, my aunt noticed me and gripped my arm.

    "You're finally here!" She trembled as she clutched at me, bringing my face close to hers, her breath hot and stale. "Where is your father? Why isn't he here yet? He should be here."

    "He'll be here tomorrow evening," I said, leaning back. "It was the earliest flight he could get. I'm sorry Big Goh-Moh."

    "How can the eldest son not be here for the death of his father?" She shook my arm. I knew I had to remain respectful, but how could she not understand that the flight alone would take fourteen hours? Perhaps if she called Toronto once in a while she would be aware of the thirteen hour time change. My father got the news just two hours ago. The family had always thought my father had shirked on his responsibilities by emigrating to Canada. Even when we ate instant noodles for a week, my parents had sent at least $500 to Seoul every month for the past thirty-five years. But that was easily overlooked when appearance was more important than substance. My mother never cooked my grandfather's meals, my aunt did. My father did not bring my grandfather under his roof to take care of him when dementia set in, my uncle did. My father was not at the hospital, but all my aunts and uncles were.

"He's coming as soon as he can, Big Goh-Moh," was all I could say before she released my arm and returned to wailing on the floor.

SUSAN PERRY

Lazarus in Heels

Synopsis
We only have one life. Or do we? Lazarus in Heels *is a novel of three interwoven stories, spanning eighty years, which demonstrate the opportunity for a second life whilst addressing the importance of friendship, the nature of gender and identity, and the search for happiness.*

Part I: MIKA
The story of a young boy's journey into reluctant manhood, starting in 1940s post-war Milan. **Mika** *isn't the same as his contemporaries: he should have been a girl. Central to this difficult coming of age narrative is the enduring bond between* **Mika** *and his boyhood friend* **Carlo**, *that sustains him through a life he never wanted, to the one he was meant to have.*

Part II: KATE
It's 2018. **Kate** *is fifty, recently widowed and stuck in a rut in Cape Town. Raising her head above the parapet of grief, she finds she's lost herself along the way. Meanwhile, her father-in-law* **Carlo** *receives an invitation from his dearest friend* **Madelina** *to attend her planned death in Milan.* **Kate** *hasn't met* **Madelina** *and knows nothing about her. Besides, does she want to be witness to another death so soon? But it's now or never to start over, so she agrees to join* **Carlo** *on this strange trip.*

Part III: MADELINA
Kate *and* **Carlo** *arrive at an edgy cultural venue in Milan run by the enigmatic, feisty but ailing* **Madelina**. *Diagnosed with dementia,* **Madelina** *is terrified her memory will trick her into reliving her previous life as* **Mika**, *and will do anything to prevent this.* **Kate** *and* **Carlo** *wrestle with the moral complexities surrounding* **Madelina**'s *desire to control her death as she controlled her life. In parallel,* **Kate** *begins her own journey of renewal.* **Madelina**'s *death reveals the extraordinary depths to which love and friendship go, including doing time for manslaughter…*

Part I: MIKA
Milan 1948
Chapter One

Carlo had been Mika's closest friend for over three years, since the Ciencento family had arrived in Via Marcetti. The unusually blonde, tall youngster seemed to enjoy the role of Mika's sidekick and protector. It suited them. Both were only children and had taken on brotherhood as a natural right, so their daytimes were filled with shouts and knuckle fives and the camaraderie of street and school. Loneliness came to Mika at night, when the moon slid across the attic ceiling lighting the emptiness of the spare bed to the far left of the room. Living in the same street meant it was a rare occasion that Carlo slept over, so no child form had etched fraternity on the sheets and no rustling giggles signified a mischievous after-hours extension into night-time explorations. Once Mika had said to Mama that perhaps a sister or a brother would be fun. But only the once. He had seen such sadness bear down over her whole body and she left the room without speaking. Papa had gone after her. Mika felt bad for having made Mama so sad and that night he tied the drawstring of his pyjama bottoms too tight so that he couldn't breathe properly or sleep. In the morning he carried shadows under his eyes and the imprint of rope around his waist.

Carlo was the next best thing to a real brother. He was a head taller and probably the same in width. His smile was wider still and his nature was as gentle and welcoming as a light breeze on one of Milan's hottest summer days. His parents had lost all their belonging in the bombings and had to work hard to catch up, so were not quite as well-to-do as Mika's. But they were undeniably of good heart. Carlo's Mama had to work and was a stenographer at Lenti's Furniture Manufacturers. At 5pm every evening her heel-savers pre-announced her arrival, with the regularity of a clock-on, clock-off worker. Tick-tacking along the cobbles, metal to stone, metal to stone, as if typing a letter with no full stops. The boys could tell whether Carlo's supper would be scratch by the speed of the clicks; a busy day and the pace was slower - it would be cold boiled eggs, cheese and bread on the table for dinner. An easier day gave energy between leather sole and street so maybe veal Milanese and fried potatoes.

But possibly the very best thing was Carlo's Papa's job. Signor Ciencento was a watch mender at the local department store and Carlo had grown up with the store as his second home, but for Mika it was a wonderous place to visit; a traditional old building with three floors of panelled oak and high ceilings. Deep red carpets hushed their awed voices, and the bell boy would let them press the brass buttons and pull the shiny lever to start and stop the lift on the required floor. Mika loved these visits. It felt grand. It smelt good. Whenever Carlo was off delivering whatever message he had to deliver to his father, Mika would visit his most favourite place in the world, the fabrics floor. Sliding between the elegant signorinas fingering taffeta and silk for dream wedding dresses, squeezing through the smaller spaces left between the tables and racks of furnishing fabrics by older, better upholstered signoras and finding his spot among the velvets, hastily stroking each roll at face level or below, searching for the softest of them all. Carlo would know to find him nestled by the aqua or aubergine crushed Florentine velvet, and would punch him hard, unsure of what to say. But Carlo liked cold tea and being strangled until he nearly passed out, which was also strange, so they said nothing and grew taller together. Carlo just did that bit rather faster than Mika.

Mika heard his mother shouting and did his best to ignore her by studiously turning to tuck in the flap of his shirt hanging over his shorts, from when Carlo and Luca had tried to snatch at him before he had outrun them. He had no trouble in eluding them because he was so fast. He'd overheard Mama telling Signora Agnelli that her boy had the speed and nimbleness of a gazelle. Even at ten years old he was showing promise in the school team and Signor Galetti had promised Mika a place in the Under 13s by next year if he continued to apply himself. Although it had not gone unnoticed that the sports master had a habit of populating his teams with the more delicately featured, fine-boned of his younger students. Gossip around the matter elicited that the more liberal parents were suggesting that the personal preference determining this selection strategy was perhaps to the detriment of the school's league performance. It was said there had been talk about Signor Galetti being moved to Santa Augusta della Souria, the girls' convent school in the adjoining district. But Mika was undeniably fast and, fine-boned or not, he was confident that he would still be selected to grace the wing of the Under-13s.

His mama's voice cut through the light Sunday morning air.

"Mika! It's time to change for church."

He knew he could not avoid the inevitable, and neither could the other boys. Religion was timetabled as seriously as school in their neighbourhood so, with grumbling and regret, the game broke up by mutual agreement with some friendly, gentle play-fighting between the four boys. Mika sloped as slowly as possible towards the front door, dragging both his feet and his discarded, dusty cardigan.

Half an hour later, Mika was suited, solemn and somnolent, sitting on the parlour settee cradling a book and praying hard that he looked tired enough that his parents wouldn't make him go. He had better things to do than spend an hour in the cold, dank confines of the church under the judgemental eye of Father Bruno, waiting to cement his mouth shut with a dry communion wafer and then release it with bitter wine. His languid but sufficiently godly demeanour was enough to prompt Mama, already in her church hat and coat, to pick up on his apparent exhaustion and utter the words he'd been hoping for.

"Mika, you're looking tired and pale. Are you sickening?"

Because it was Sunday and God was all-knowing, Mika made a hasty judgment not to lie, said nothing and coughed lightly. It had the desired effect. Mama decisively announced that Mika would be attending only evensong that day.

"The child is definitely coming down with something. He does not look well and the Lord has given us glorious sunshine for healing. Go change, and take some sunshine in the park. But no football. You've played enough this morning. In fact I think you may have overdone it and that's the reason for your pallor. You can stay home, rest and reflect. You may not be in church, but it's still the Lord's Day."

Mika smiled his thanks, but mindful of his spurious incubating illness took the stairs slowly up to his bedroom to change.

As he reached the top landing, Mika could hear Mama in the hallway snippily informing Papa that there would always be time to offer up their souls to the Lord even if they had much to repent, and double that to give thanks for.

He waited until he was sure the house was his. Carefully opening the door to his mother's dark oak closet, he stood, silent for a moment. Considering.

Despite, or perhaps because of her somewhat erratic temperament, she kept her cupboards well ordered, whether they contained provisions, linen, or clothing. Blouses to the top rail. Skirts to the bottom. A rail for full length items to the rear. Scarves hung from a makeshift loop of silken rope to the inside of the door. Hats which did not have their own boxes sat sullenly in their everydayness on the top shelf. Footwear was neatly lined up in the bottom, in three rows from front to back, pedestrian through to glamorous. Pushing his hands through the centre of first the blouses and then the skirts, he slid them along the rails to left and right revealing Mama's dresses equally neatly ordered. He ran the tips of his fingers across the fabrics with his eyes closed, as if reading colours and patterns in braille. He passed quickly over the plain and polka dot everyday cotton dresses, slowing to enjoy the soft fine woollen pinafores, and hastened over the military style tweeds kept for winter funerals or other ecclesiastical events, before reaching the flowing, silky, polyester dresses, their status for special occasions signified by bows, snippets of lace or elegant tiny matching material buttons. Here he lingered.

He hated the utilitarian look and feel of his shorts. They were ugly and rough against his skin. The colours were plain and dark. Oh how he envied Mama and the whole of womenkind the colour and variety of their wardrobes. She could change her appearance with a touch of blush and a carefully draped scarf. He just didn't understand why he couldn't do the same. He'd never asked to try Mama's lipstick again after Papa cuffed him hard round the head; he'd only been about six or seven, but even then he'd been hungry for beauty, hungry to try the things that he now realised were far out of the reach of a young boy.

He loathed the muscular look of his legs, slender but taut and bulging from football practice. Despite himself he grew stronger and faster every year. In this, his eleventh year, he'd grown nearly two inches, and there seemed to be nothing he could do to stop it. He had rubbed at the fine dark hair that was showing in various places on his body because he needed to keep his skin smooth like Mama's. His feet felt too big for the size of his body. His penis confused him with its inner life seemingly so detached from his own, and he deeply resented the fact that it seemed to be the one body part that God had chosen to publicly demonstrate innocent joy. Just last week he had felt the sun on his face and while the warmth opened his chest to give space to his heart, this autonomous appendage had stiffened and pushed insistently against the cotton lining of his underpants leading him to hide in shame. Why were these things happening to him? He could see there was an alternative and he wanted it. How he wanted it.

His bedroom window overlooked the street and he spent hours watching the girls below, skirts ballooning in the wind with glorious abandon as they played hopscotch with stones on the pavement, giggling and unknowingly free. His father would come into the bedroom from time to time to find Mika gazing longingly, and with a gruff harrumph would back out, looking approving and smiling knowingly. Did he *know*? Did Papa know how he felt? Surely he would be horrified, not pleased. Mika watched as each summer turned to autumn when cardigans would cover dresses stretching across tomboy torsos transitioning to budding girlhood. Some would grow tall and elegant like Mama, and others would grow rounder, softer and bosomy like their mothers. But none of them would have to carry these feelings of confusion, frustration and unhappiness. Each one would rise like a phoenix from the flames of adolescence, vibrant, colourful, showy and adorned, while he was consigned and constrained to live his life trapped and grey. But in Mama's room, here in front of Mama's wardrobe, whenever he had the house to himself and for one hour on this Sunday in May, he could be free too.

What he was doing was most probably sinful. In fact he knew it must be, because he'd never spoken about it. But nothing felt more right and pure than his image reflected back at him from Mama's full length oak swing mirror as he smoothed the floral-patterned artificial silk over his hips.

As a result of his absence, Mika was not to know that Father Bruno was on vacation and there was a substitute priest who clearly felt that a break from fire and brimstone might be welcomed, so the service was a good half hour shorter than usual. Mika had put a record on the gramophone player, and the sweet tenor notes of the operatic score masked the sound of the front door opening and closing. The aria soared over his mother's footsteps on the stair.

Mika was modelling one of her shorter dresses, buttons undone at the back, underskirt splayed above his knees. A cut from a boot stud sullied his shin. A large bruise on his upper left arm glowed mustard yellow, showing its age. He had laid out a longer skirt and chiffon top with sequins on the bed in readiness. Around his neck was the bright, patterned, silky scarf that Papa had given her for Christmas last year. His toes thrust over the end of her purple silk mules with the pompoms on the front. He had his back to her but he could see her enter the room behind him in the mirror. He had oiled his hair back with pomade and used her lipstick and rouge with surprising restraint and delicacy. He was holding his arms out sideways, twisting at the waist with one knee turned inwards in a pseudo film star pose.

A guttural sound unlike anything he had ever heard before wrested itself from his mother's throat and she stepped away as if propelled backwards toward the staircase without any control over her limbs. Self preservation or maternal instinct made her turn and swiftly pull the door to block Silvano's line of sight, but it was too late.

CAROLINE PRICE

Martha Dunn

Synopsis
Martha Dunn *is a contemporary literary mystery set in France about an Englishwoman who frees herself from a damaging affair through immersion in a stranger's story.*

When Martha, a 34-year-old translator, arrives in the Camargue in December 2007 to begin a residency at the Association des Angles – known for its prize for a story celebrating the local bullfighting culture – her thoughts are still dominated by the abusive, married colleague she's escaped from by coming here. She rebuffs everyone around her, including her co-resident Gilles, a French author who tries to befriend her, and immerses herself in her work. But when she's given a manuscript by a previous elderly resident, Pierre, who died suddenly before he could submit it for the prize, she finds herself absorbed by his story and decides to finish it on his behalf.

Pierre's story (alternating with the contemporary text) tells of a schoolteacher's concern for a pupil, maltreated by his bullfighter father, who disappeared following a tragedy in 1958 in which many bulls died. The story reveals that not only was the teacher the boy's real father but that Pierre himself was the teacher, returning fifty years later to give a voice to his forgotten son. While here, Pierre encountered a former pupil, Émile, who implied he knew the truth about the boy's disappearance, but died before he could challenge him.

Martha confronts Émile herself, and learns that the boy drowned accidentally; but Émile, fearing repercussions if the story is told, behaves threateningly and she is grateful to be rescued unexpectedly by Gilles. Gilles takes her to Nîmes to distract her; during the evening, as they eat and then ice-skate together, she gradually opens up to him and although his residency is over, they tentatively discuss a future where she might translate his work.

MIDI LIBRE LE GAILLARD   September 18th 2009

*Rhône-Sète Canal: **Mystery of human remains
at pumping station***
Late last Tuesday afternoon, residents of Les Angles were surprised to see several police cars making their way towards the Pont de la Padelle on the Rhône-Sète Canal, where the pumping station is currently undergoing reconstruction work. The police had been called to the scene by one of the workmen, still in shock after having discovered, wedged inside an old drainage pipe beneath the station, remains which were unmistakeably human...

* * *

DECEMBER 2007

Valence, we will shortly be arriving in Valence. Please be aware that the train will stop for three minutes only ...

Martha shifted herself upright and half-opened her eyes. The Frenchman seated opposite who had tried once or twice during the journey to engage her in conversation was getting to his feet, looping his scarf around his neck. He caught her gaze and smiled. 'Just time for a ciggy ...'

She let her eyelids drop, burying herself back into her seat. The train slowed and slid to a halt in a long exhalation of breath. The odours of coffee and unwrapped food washed round her as people jostled along the aisle; the automatic doors pumped a stale draught through the compartment as they opened and closed. Other passengers were boarding; she could hear them dragging their baggage past, sense them hesitating as they searched for their places.

She turned her head to the window, rested her forehead against the glass, re-opened one eye. Laden figures pushed in both directions on the platform, agitated after the long delay. Her neighbour was standing near the carriage door, motionless in the confusion, muffled in his scarf. The glowing tip of his cigarette moved in an arc, rising and falling. Smoke rose around him like breath.

A guard passed the window, and within a few seconds the drawn-out shriek of a whistle pierced the air. Her neighbour lifted his head; a last inhale and he dropped the half-smoked cigarette, ground it quickly underfoot.

Moments later he was inside again, shrugging off his jacket and folding it into the rack above their heads. As he slid back into his seat he glanced at her. 'It's not snowing here. This is the south!'

Martha closed her eyes again, erasing him.

The snow had arrived during the night, as had been forecast: unusually severe weather for the beginning of December, flakes already falling thickly as she left Wood Green just after six that morning, enough by the time she reached Waterloo to merge pavements with roads even in the centre of the city. Eurostar trains were being cancelled or rescheduled; instead of the three hours and lunch in Paris she had anticipated, she was propelled into a race against the clock to the Gare de Lyon, crushed with damp-coated crowds on the suburban line, willing the train to keep going, dragging her suitcase along corridors and down and up stairs to the eventual icy above-ground air and flickering notice boards, ramming her ticket into the punching machine while the station announcements rang in her ears: her TGV was still scheduled, thank God, it was there waiting now. She'd half run, half stumbled along the platform to her carriage and hauled her case inside, wedging it somehow into a space in the luggage compartment. When she finally let go of the handle her fingers were rigid, her body trembling. Five minutes later the train pulled out of its glass and steel shed into an utterly white landscape.

The snow was if anything thicker in France. A blanket thrown to the horizon, no distinction between land and sky; a scene without sound. Snow ploughs pushed their way along country roads. The weather must have closed the schools: on the slopes around the towns, children raced downhill on sledges, black stick figures spread-eagled against white. The train slowed, halted, moved forward in staggered bursts before picking up speed again. Somewhere south of Dijon, a strained voice made an announcement. *This train is running approximately fifty minutes late, we apologise for the delay which is due to exceptional weather conditions across the country ...*

An excuse to switch on her phone. Holding it buried in her lap, she'd typed a quick message for the woman who was due to pick her up in Nîmes: Sorry but train from Paris delayed, will keep you in touch ...

Some minutes later a text came through in reply: OK, no problem.

There were no other new messages for her. She turned the phone off and dropped it into her bag, leaned her head back against the hard fabric headrest. No, Martha. Focus on why you're here, what you've come here to do. What you want to do.

She must have made a sound; the young Frenchman sitting opposite her had glanced at her and then glanced again, his eyes brightening.

She tightened her lips with a frown and turned to gaze out of the window, at the white, featureless landscape sliding past. How mean she was. And how little she cared.

The hours passed; afternoon deepened to dusk, dusk to darkness. The Frenchman left the train at Orange without a word or another glance. Martha dozed, read, dozed off again; must have entered a deeper sleep at last because when she opened her eyes, abruptly, people in the carriage were stirring, packing their belongings away, doing up their coats. She cupped her hand against her face to block her own reflection and stared out of the window into the night. Nothing; just the occasional light of a building, one or two, then a few more; trees between them, the branches darker against the dark sky. No sign of any conurbation, yet – but a moment later the public address system crackled into life. *Nîmes, we will shortly be arriving in Nîmes where this train will now terminate. We apologise for the disruption to this journey and thank you for your patience. Passengers for Montpellier and Narbonne should go to platform six ...*

Everyone was standing now, swaying and leaning around her. She let them do what they wanted, waited until the queue had shuffled past to jam itself at the end of the carriage before rising stiffly to her own feet. Where had her coat got to, her scarf ... Despite the sleep she was giddy with tiredness. She pushed back her sleeve to peer at her watch: a quarter to eight. Even with the hour's difference she had been travelling for almost thirteen hours. But she was here; she had done it. The knowledge was abstract; she was too tired even to feel relief.

Her suitcase was toppled on its side where others propping it up had been removed. She dragged it upright and hauled it down the steep step onto the platform, fumbled for its handle, followed the throng of people towards the exit. The platforms were enclosed, seemed interminable. Eventually she was funnelled through the barrier with the rest, everyone spreading out then, hurrying in their different directions. She continued forward for a few paces, stopped and let the crowds flow around her and on until she was almost alone in the middle of the dimly lit concourse. The exit next to the Avia car hire office, that was what she had to look for. She gazed round until she saw the signs, started pulling her case towards them.

A woman detached herself from the shadows, moved towards her. 'Martha, Martha Dunn? . . I thought it must be you!' She held out her hand. 'I'm Léa Blanchard.'

Her voice was bright, her ungloved hand warm. She was wearing a red coat against which her haze of fair curls when she turned looked almost white. 'Come this way, I've parked just outside …'

Martha staggered behind her, her case bumping over the ridged rubber flooring. 'I'm sorry I'm so late,' she murmured. 'The weather, in London and then in Paris …'

'Yes, I know. All the snow!' Léa Blanchard pushed through a glass door and then another, holding them open. 'It doesn't matter, it's not serious, a couple of hours, that's all. I just left two hours later than I would have done.'

The doors swung closed behind them; they were outside, in a wide paved area facing a road pulsing with traffic, noise, lights. The air was cold and dry. Martha paused, took a deep breath. 'There's no snow here.'

The other woman laughed. 'No, we don't often see snow, in this part of France! There's a point where it stops – '

'At Valence.'

'Yes, around Valence!' She crossed the pavings to a row of parked vehicles, opened the door of a small silver car. 'Here we are, can you manage your case …'

As they pulled away she glanced at Martha, slumped back in the passenger seat. 'It's a long journey, from England. You must be tired.'

Martha nodded. 'Yes.'

They slid into the river of cars.

There was so much traffic, even at this hour; she hadn't expected it. Horns blared sharply, a frenzy of red, orange and yellow lights pressed at her half-closed eyelids. 'Is it always like this, so busy?' she murmured eventually, turning her head without raising it.

Her companion switched lanes and then back again. 'Oh yes, Nîmes is a busy place, it's expanded so much, so many people live and work here now … ' She was driving quickly, confidently; she braked sharply at a roundabout, shot across. 'But where you're going … Even Le Gaillard, Le Gaillard is very different …'

Traffic lights brought her to a halt. 'You've not visited this region before?'

'No … Well, Arles, once, but a long time ago …'

Martha didn't want to talk; she felt too exhausted. She wanted only to arrive, to shut the door, to be in her own space. But there was this journey still to be negotiated. She had to make an effort.

The other woman was laughing again. 'But you must be very familiar with France. You speak French so well. That's unusual!'

'Not really. It's my subject.'

Her voice sounded distant, not like her own. She made herself continue, less harshly. 'I grew up in France ... My father worked in France, in Normandy ... We lived in Normandy, I went to school there, primary school ...'

She could be talking about someone else entirely. The words hung disembodied, juddering as the lights changed and the engine surged again.

'Then it'll be quite simple for you, talking to the students tomorrow –' The young woman broke off for a moment to take a filter lane. 'I did mention that you have a meeting tomorrow?'

'Tomorrow?' She couldn't keep the sharpness out of her voice. 'No, I didn't know.'

'Yes ... I hope that will suit you, I had to rearrange it at the last minute, for tomorrow morning, it was the only option, before the students finish their term. It's at a Lycée in Nîmes, you'll be coming back to Nîmes, but I'll bring you here and drive you back again ... It's not until eleven thirty, just a one-hour meeting, a chance to talk with the students, an opportunity for them to ask you questions, it'll be very straightforward, and pleasant ...'

Her voice pattered on, brightly and enthusiastically. Martha let what she was saying wash over her. Tomorrow morning, did it really matter, she was too tired to think about it now. Outside, junctions and roundabouts and blocks of illuminated apartments gave way to suburbs which in turn faded to matt darkness dotted with individual lights. The tail lamps of the vehicle in front loomed, disappeared, were replaced by others: Léa Blanchard overtook easily, completely familiar with the route. Martha gazed out of the window without focusing; her head felt too heavy to move. Impossible to imagine that this morning she'd woken up in her own bed, in snow-blanketed England, had washed her face in her own bathroom ... How dirty her face must be now, how dusty, how sweaty she must be, how much she wanted to arrive, to sink down in a room alone, to be able to be silent, to gather herself ...

MARGARET SESSA-HAWKINS

Migratory Patterns

Synopsis
Migratory Patterns *tells the story of Grace, an American girl who grows up in Malawi. As with many transnational bildungsroman, the plot focuses on Grace situating herself in the world as she grows, with the narrative exploring themes of identity, belonging, and acceptance. However, the novel breaks with the genre in several key aspects.*

The first way in which Migratory Patterns *diverges from similar works is its focus on female characters — Grace's bond with her two best friends, Tamanda and Mercy, is the driving force of the narrative. This friendship serves as a form of home for Grace, and is meant to contrast with the frequent literary positioning of romances as the most meaningful interaction a woman can have.*

The second way in which the narrative diverges from other migratory fictions is in Grace's strong attachment to both the United States and Malawi. In this way, Grace is representative of a growing global population that view themselves as fully transnational — with an intrinsic part of her identity linked to more than one country. It is Grace's struggle to maintain this connection to two places she loves deeply that provides the novel's main conflict.

The third way the novel differs from many contemporaries is its exploration of specific environments over general geographies. Within Migratory Patterns, *each chapter is set in a significant natural area. In this way, Grace's sense of place is not just a cultural or political matter, but also an inherently environmental one, and environmental destruction is portrayed as a colonial but also deeply personal self-destructive act.*

In diverging from other works in this way, Migratory Patterns *aims to be not just a book that focuses on migration — it aims to examine migration as one part of a larger and more holistic story about a girl's life.*

Prologue

The night after her father's funeral, Grace cannot sleep. She lies, curled into the shape of a comma on the guest bed in her mother's house, and finds that her eyes will not close. She slept fine the night her father died. She came home from the hospital that evening with her mother, lay down on this same guest bed, and collapsed into a deep oblivion. She has slept perfectly every night since then, dozing off easily each evening around nine. She can see by the haggard looks her mother and brother and aunt wear each morning that the same is not true for them. Grace has felt, looking at their bruised eyes and sagging faces, that they are processing their grief in a way that is healthier, more appropriate than her. But tonight – after a lovely service, after connecting with so many people, after receiving all those heartfelt condolences – John and her mother and her Aunt Meredith are finally resting. It is only Grace who cannot sleep.

Her mother has gone full Maine on this room. There is a watercolor of a quiet cove to Grace's left, a photograph of a loon on a lake to her right, an old poster depicting all the buoys of the Monhegan Island lobstermen at the head of the bed. Strangest of all, there is a large crocheted moose head above the door. The head is even mounted on a board and hung up the way a real trophy would be. The only non-Maine artifact in the entire room is the photograph at the foot of Grace's bed. It shows three women, silhouetted against the rising sun, large baskets balanced on their heads. The photograph is from Malawi. Grace took it years ago, when she was maybe ten or eleven, back when her whole family lived in a small village in the country.

The photograph was not here the last time Grace visited her parents. Grace wonders when they decided to hang it up, and why. She will have to ask. In the morning, maybe, or possibly even later, maybe in a few days. Grace hears a creak from outside the room, and tilts her head back to see her brother, leaning easily against the frame of the door.

"I thought you were finally getting some sleep," she says, rolling over to face him.

"I was," John shrugs. "But I woke up about twenty minutes ago and realized that was it for tonight." He raises his eyebrows and she scoots back, making room for him on the bed. He curls up opposite her, his feet by her head, so they lie together like yin and yang. He stares at the crocheted moose head. "Is it strange that I find that a bit creepy?" He asks. Grace laughs. "I mean, it is weird to imagine Mom with a hunting rifle, don't you think? To think of her out in those yarn forests, stalking stuffed hares, trying to trap a threaded turkey, pursuing a plushie pheasant." Grace shakes her head and hits him gently on the shin. He sits up slightly and faces her. "I am serious Grace! She could have come across a knitted bear! What then?"

Grace wipes away the remnants of tears from her cheeks. "You are terrible," she tells him. He laughs and rolls over, staring up at the ceiling.

"Remember when you used to have stars in your room? When we were children and you plastered glow-in-the-dark plastic stars all over the ceiling?" He asks. Grace can feel the vibration of the words as he speaks, as he chuckles slightly.

"Of course," Grace smiles. She remembers getting the stars for her birthday, peeling the thin plastic backings off them one by one, and sticking them onto the ceiling, trying as best she could to replicate the actual night sky. "I loved them so much," she says, wistful. "When Mom and Dad moved back to America I tried to peel them down and take them along."

"No dice?"

"Nope. They just fell apart."

John props himself up on his elbow, looking down at her. "How would you feel about getting out of here?" He asks.

"What about Mom?"

"She's still asleep. I can leave her a note, tell her to call if she gets worried." He raises his eyebrows. "Come on. What do you say?"

"What the hell," Grace shrugs with a certain resignation, and rolls out of the bed, shivering as her bare feet hit the wooden floorboards. "Just give me a few minutes to grab my coat and boots."

* * *

John has not said where they are going, and Grace does not care enough to ask. They have been in the car for about a half an hour, they are driving south, they are using the small winding backroads that crisscross the state. That is all she knows. In the glass of the car window she can see her own reflection, spectral. She is draped in the black dress she wore to the funeral, loose around her frame, and she has on thick stockings, with her legs crossed on the seat beneath her.

"Okay?" John asks, motioning to the temperature gauge on the dash.

"Perfect," Grace confirms.

Outside the car, the air around them is thick and black. The moon, half-full in the sky, set hours ago, and there are no street lamps on these winding country lanes. John's headlights, flipped to high beams, shine bright white on the asphalt before them, on the thin veil of fog in the air, on the trees that cluster tightly around them on either side. The geographic history of Maine is one of ice. The hills and valleys through which they now drive were sculpted by it, millions of years ago. When Grace first heard this fact, back when she was four or maybe five, she found it hard to believe. The idea of glaciers moving across the land, scouring slabs of granite as they went, carrying boulders along in their wake, shearing off entire mountaintops, it was incredible. Looking out now though, across the dark night, she can see it. She can easily envision everything around them encased in frozen sheets, thousands of feet deep.

John's watch beeps. Grace stares at the clock on the dash, which shows that it is just now five-nineteen, and tries to figure out why John would have an alarm set.

"It is astronomical dawn," he says softly.

"What?"

"Astronomical dawn," John points out the windshield. "It means it is no longer completely dark outside. There is a little bit of light."

Grace stares out through the windshield. "I cannot see any difference," she says.

"I know," John stretches slightly, rolling his shoulders and flexing his fingers against the steering wheel. "But there is one."

He leans over and flips on the radio. A slow melody, picked out on a mandolin, floats through the car. John starts humming along softly with the chords, gently tapping his fingers on the edge of the steering wheel in time with the tune. A violin solo takes over, and Grace leans back and rests her head against her seat. She knows where they are going now. A while ago, the landscape began to materialize into familiar shapes, forest interrupted by flat black swathes that look like clear patches of prairie but are actually the glassy surfaces of small lakes and ponds. Grace recognizes this area, remembers her father saying – as a throwaway thought maybe a year ago – that someday they should go to Cadillac Mountain and watch the sun rise. That in the winter it was the first place in the northeast where the sun came up. That it would be something to see, wouldn't it? And they all agreed that it would and then they all forgot about it, just like that.

Ahead of them, Grace can barely make out the vague outline of the Trenton Bridge. It is still small in the distance, passing low over the Mount Desert Narrows. Even from so far though, Grace can see the broad contours of Mount Desert Island – the thick blanket of pines, the stark and jagged coastline, the rising peak of Cadillac Mountain. Leaning back in her seat, Grace closes her eyes. She can picture so clearly the familiar sights of Acadia National Park – the deep pink groves of blooming rhododendron, the hiking trails winding through dense forests, the clear waters of Jordan Pond.

Just a few months ago they were there, the entire family, on a day trip they took right before it became fully spring. The air was full of a crisp cold and they wrapped up in hats and gloves and scarves and wore thick down jackets. They took bikes and rode along the gravel paths of the old carriage roads and absorbed every detail of the glittering snow-bitten landscape around them. Her father kept goofing around, taking his hands off the handlebars and trying to balance. "Look at me!" He would yell, his arms raised high in the air, the bike weaving uncontrollably underneath him. "Look what I can do!"

* * *

The darkness has almost faded by the time they reach the mountaintop. In its place a pale blue pre-dawn light illuminates the granite crags, the tessellations of lichen and the clumps of rough shrubbery that sprout from the rocky gaps. Grace has her jacket and boots and hat and gloves back on. It is cold, but pleasantly so. Around them, the ground and the leaves sparkle with hoar frost, and their breath hangs in the chill of the air. John has set up two folding chairs near the edge of the mountaintop. Grace and John sit on the canvas surfaces, heavy fleece blankets tucked around them, and look out. There are small crowds gathered all along the peak, drawn by the promise of prime fall foliage and a breathtaking landscape illuminated by the dawn light. Several groups have decided to picnic. They have got wicker baskets unfolded in front of them. They have tiny plates and cups and silverware laid out before them. They are eating small muffins, and mini-quiches, and fruit salads. They are drinking mimosas from thin glass flutes.

"Want any?" John asks, picking a thermos up from his side, unscrewing a small plastic mug from its top and offering it to Grace.

"What is it?"

"Spiced apple cider," John tells her. Grace nods, and John loosens the top of the thermos, and then pours the steaming liquid into her cup; she can smell the apples, the cinnamon, the cloves. Her first sip, the kick hits her hard. She comes up coughing and sputtering.

"Brandy," she manages to choke out. "You spiked the apple cider with brandy. You bastard." John grins, and takes slow sips of his own drink. Prepared now, Grace sips again. The cider is smooth, and sharp, and she feels the warmth of the added alcohol settle gently in her stomach. Gradually, a pleasant ease stretches through her limbs. John is looking up, staring at the dark aquamarine of the sky above them. "Is that Venus?" He asks, pointing to a bright spot of light before them, one of only about five points that can still be seen in the sky.

"Yup," Grace confirms.

"What about that one?" He indicates a much dimmer point of light, off to the right of Venus.

"Sirius," Grace tells him, and then, preemptively, "You can see Rigel just over there," she motions further to the right of Sirius. "And there is Betelgeuse," she points to the star just above and to the left of Rigel.

John shakes his head. "That is really quite cool." He tells her.

Grace has always been obsessed with astronomy, ever since she was young. She was forever wandering off into fields and staring up at the blanket of the heavens above her. By the time she was ten, she could name all the constellations. Not just the easy ones, like the Big Dipper and the Little Dipper and Orion and Pegasus. She knew Auriga and Cassiopeia and even Camelopardalis, the giraffe. She made her parents buy her Ptolemy's *Almagest*. For years she logged in to internet cafes in the city just to look at photographs from Hubble.

The rest of her family never really got into it, but her father liked that she liked space. He went along with her to the fields. He helped her to set up her telescope. He helped her to puzzle through star charts, and got her posters of planets and galaxies and supernovas to hang on her wall. He bought her the glow-in-the-dark plastic stars for her birthday. He helped her decide what patterns she should follow when putting them up. They drew out the designs on grid paper together.

And now her father is gone.

Grace takes another deep sip of her cider. On a long inhale, she looks out before them, taking in the entirety of the mountaintop. There is more light now. Out on the ocean, she can just make out the crests of waves and currents as they form and beat against the shore. Next to her, John is silent, and Grace feels they are both probably lost in the scenery, and the soft chatter of the groups around them, and their own particular thoughts.

John still does not say anything, but carefully he reaches down and removes a glove, extending his bare hand out to her, palm up. After a beat, Grace removes her own glove, reaches down as well, and laces her fingers in his. In the cool of the air around them she can still feel the warmth of his palm against hers.

Grace blinks rapidly, and then wipes her hand across her eyes, brushing away the small traces of moisture that have settled there. In front of them, there is a glow at the base of the horizon, a strong yellow light just above the waters of the ocean. Soon, Grace knows, the heavens will be streaked with ochre and crimson and rose. Soon, she knows, the colors will return to the earth and they will be able to see the blue of the sound, the green of the pines, the deep fire of the autumn leaves around them. Soon, she knows, the sun will come up and its light will wash over them. For now though she sits, hand in hand with John, and, like everyone else on the mountain top, looks out toward the east, waiting for the sun to rise.

LIZ SKITT

Small Thief

Synopsis
Surrounded by wealth that isn't his, Hugh enjoys a game of petty theft until one disastrous mistake leads to the death of a friend. Haunted by remorse, he accepts a challenge – set a thief to catch a thief – and heads off halfway across the world to try and stop a crime.

In the late 1980s, repulsed by the wealth and violence he witnesses as a scholarship boy at a remote Scottish private school, Hugh retaliates through stealing from those around him: the protection racket he sets up with his friend, Hyder, has classmates paying the school thief to save their possessions from the school thief.

When he meets Julia on his year abroad from Oxford and moves with her to Leipzig, he experiences a new sense of freedom, all certainties shredded by the bubbling possibilities of a city emerging from Communism. He befriends his neighbour Josef and becomes fascinated by Josef's GDR secrets. He also meets Wolf, a money-obsessed banker who is instantly attracted to Julia.

As Hugh and Julia's relationship disintegrates and she leaves him for Wolf, Hugh drowns his sorrows with Josef, expressing the wish that he had grown up under Communism's level playing field. This finally provokes Josef to tell of his imprisonment in the GDR and terror of the police. When Hugh arrives home from pawning a necklace that Julia left behind, he finds Julia and Wolf shouting threats to call the police outside Josef's door. As he pleads with them to stop, they hear a body fall outside.

Years later, Hugh accepts a challenge from his old friend Hyder and travels to Argentina, there discovering that his own shame is the key that can unlock a hidden world of greed and corruption.

CHAPTER 1: Harpleton
A boy slapped his lunch tray down on the table opposite Hugh. "Make yourself useful," he said and immediately began twirling forkfuls of spaghetti, his actions dextrous and assured.

Hugh looked around to see if anyone was watching.

"Do something for them and they leave you alone," the boy continued. He counted on his fingers. "Get something they want. Make something disappear. Take the blame." He stopped counting. "Actually, that's it. Those are the three things you can do."

"Fetch and carry."

"You'll do that anyway." He fixed his eyes on Hugh. "And when you've done something for them and they're leaving you alone, do something for yourself." He smiled. "Makes it all better."

"Like?"

"Loads of options." He nodded in the direction of the staff table. "Most of them do something else as well as teach. Clubs, you know." He made his way down the table, wagging his fork in the direction of each teacher. "Chess. Debating. Climbing. Running. Bridge." The fork stopped. "Never French conversation practice. Got it?"

"Why?"

"Doesn't matter. And he's only here for an exchange year, so no point making a fuss." The fork continued. "Acting. Target shooting. Extra rugby. Whatever you want. Best not too academic. Might seem provocative from someone like you."

"And if I don't want to do anything for them?"

The boy put his head to one side. "Well, that would be stupid."

Hugh shrugged. "Who are you anyway?"

"Skids."

"And your real name?"

The boy looked surprised. "Hyder."

"And which do you prefer?"

A ball of spaghetti grew too large. Skids rejected it and started another. "Hyder," he considered, "but it doesn't work here. People mess with names too much. 'Jeckell' was good while it lasted. But it was always going to be Heidi in the end."

"Except that you're Skids."

"And you are?" Everyone knew Hugh's nickname. The question was a chalk line on the ground. My pain; yours. Don't cross. "You're a day boy, right?"

"Yeah."

"So you go home every night? To the village."

"Course."

"Then get me three litres of vodka. By Saturday. And I'll let it be known that you're in."

Hugh shovelled his soup, thinking. The conversation meant nothing, probably. They'd never speak again, most likely. But he was enjoying the novelty of thoughts turning into sounds. It was making him feel quite lightheaded.

Small Thief

"Chess is my gig," Hyder continued. "I can checkmate most people in ten moves."

"Yeah?"

"Can teach you, if you like."

"OK."

"And you're eating that all wrong. Fill the soup spoon away from your body," Hyder mimed it. "Don't shovel it towards you."

"Right."

"I'll give you money when we get back to the house."

* * *

Hugh's village could be mapped like a family tree: five thousand people and a handful of surnames, blood lines leading back to your door. The people in the off-licence would tell his mum, honesty the only policy.

He watched his mother's face as he explained: the smile when she understood that he had been asked to do a favour for a new 'friend' at the school; the twitch of doubt as she began to understand what he was asking for; the slow downward pull on her lips and eyes as if every word he spoke added more weights to the ends of invisible threads; the spasm of alarm when he held out the money Hyder had given to him.

"What have you done to your hands?"

"Nothing." He put them behind his back.

"Show me!" She grabbed one of his forearms and tried to pull it round from behind his body. "What the …?"

Hand holding. Something the bigger boys did to new boys.

"Will you get it for me?" he asked.

"What happened to your hands?"

"Will you get it for me?" He stared out the doubts on her face.

She nodded.

He dropped the money quickly on the table: a fifty-pound note. "Hyder didn't have anything smaller." As they stared at the money, the space between them in the tiny kitchen widened infinitely.

* * *

The change from that fifty was burning a hole in Hugh's pocket.

"Keep it," Hyder had said.

A pocket that was in his hand-me-down school trousers; trousers he had to keep adjusting to stop them cutting into his testicles; an adjustment noticed by all the other boys before he had been at the school for half an hour; the source of his hilarious Harpleton nickname: Scratcher.

"Something for yourself," Hyder kept reminding him. "Makes it all better."

That Saturday, they snuck out of the school grounds and made their way to the nearest town on the local bus. Sitting at the back, it was the fairground ride of his childhood: humpback bridge; sand strewn road; hairpin bend. Flat fields stretched away from them in every direction until, just beyond the edge of one of those fields, cliffs plunged to rocks and foam beneath.

"I don't think it was harshly meant," Hyder spoke above the growling of the bus, apparently mid-way through a conversation he had started in his head.

"What wasn't?"

"Skids." Hyder turned to him. "Thing is, when I'm home in London, we put our dirty clothes in a laundry basket, and they come back clean. So, when North told us at the start of my first term here to take our clothes to the laundry, I figured he meant the same thing. And I only bothered to hunt around for the basket when I started running out of stuff. Searched every inch of the boarding house."

"Why didn't you ask someone?"

"Don't know."

"And what did you do?"

"I started from the beginning again with all my clothes and I wore my underpants inside out." Hyder looked at Hugh, eyes drooping. "Went on for quite a while."

"But you still didn't ask?"

"Too late by then." Hyder turned away and stared out of the window.

"So, what happened?"

"One day a sixth former told me to take his clothes to the laundry and it was one of the better ones, you know, so I was quite pleased there was finally a chance to find out. I told him that I didn't actually know where the laundry basket was, and he asked me all the kinds of questions you've been asking me now."

"Then?"

"He put his arm round my shoulders, took me through to the common room and pulled my trousers down in front of everyone." Hyder made a noise that wasn't quite a laugh. "Was a struggle, I can tell you."

* * *

Small Thief

At three o'clock, Hugh's purchase secured, they were a few words away from being thrown out of the only electrics shop in town.

"A small acknowledgement is all I'm asking for," Hyder persisted.

"Six hundred and ninety-nine pounds and ninety-nine pence." The man's neck was turning red.

"Because I'm paying cash."

"Six hundred and ninety-nine pounds and ninety-nine pence."

Hyder took a breath.

"One more word," the man held up a hand, "and you're out on your ear."

Hyder looked at the hand and nodded. He started pulling money out of his pocket, piling crumpled twists of paper on the counter, spreading and stacking the notes. "My father taught me never to take the first price as final."

The man didn't say anything.

"But I'm a hundred quid short anyway. Or thereabouts." He turned to Hugh. "You got it?"

The casualness of the question winded Hugh. "No."

"Then, it'll have to be a cheque anyway." Hyder smiled at the man again. "I have a gold guarantee card."

"I'll take your money any way you want, son."

* * *

Hugh's body ached with curiosity as they walked to the bus station, waited in the rain, sat on the bus, made their way down the school drive and snuck back into the boarding house. He had known, of course, but it was different, seeing it in action.

"You have a lot of money," he managed to say eventually.

Hyder was unpacking his purchase. "My father. You know." He always said 'you know' as if hitting the button in timed chess. Your turn now. You go.

"No, I don't."

Hyder stopped connecting wires and flicking switches. "What don't you know?"

"Any of it. I don't have a rich father. I don't have a father."

"What happened to him?"

"He flew planes. One crashed." Hugh paused. "You know."

"Well," Hyder pressed a button and a song started, "there are pluses and minuses to the whole father thing." He raised his voice above the music, "On the plus side, mine gives North cash for me every term and I think it's more than North earns in the whole year. Which I like."

Hugh pictured the housemaster loading neat wads of notes into a safe. "Surprised he doesn't nick any."

"Doesn't need to. I ..." For a second it looked like Hyder was going to say more until he changed his mind with a shake of his head. "It wouldn't make sense. In the long run his salary will add up to more than he could steal. And my father would know."

"How?"

"That's the minus side of fathers. Or mine anyway. Knows what you're doing before you've thought of it yourself," Hyder reduced the volume of the song and his voice at the same time, whispering, "and his disappointment drains the blood from your veins."

They both laughed.

"You remember yours?" Hyder continued. The question was casual, but there was a watchfulness between them; an awareness that one or other might want an easy escape and they should be ready to grab a distraction from the air.

"Not really."

He had one memory and it was probably false. His own face in his father's shoes. Must have crawled over to them, attracted by their shininess. But he would have been too young, wouldn't he? No-one has memories from before they can walk. It must have been fed to him by someone else. He could hear his mother's voice in the background, laughing. He felt her hands around his waist, scooping him away, and that voice, "Leave him be, Nora. Let him dribble on them. I've got plenty of time." More laughter.

In the hush, a new sound: the fire door in the corridor crashed open. "Skids!"

Both boys became still.

Davis, scourge of the first years and the sixth form entrants: sprogs and bentrants as they were known. "I can smell you, Skids," the voice continued.

"Here."

"We're a man short. Grab your kit and get downstairs."

"I have a note." There was an edge of panic in Hyder's voice.

"Don't give a fuck." The older boy's head appeared around the side of the door. "Get down to the boot room." He grinned and disappeared.

"I could ...," Hugh started

"Doesn't work like that." Hyder was already kicking out of his trousers, tripping over the tangle. "See you at supper," and he was gone.

A ball of crumpled notes lay in the middle of the floor next to the pile of discarded clothes. Hugh reached down and picked it up, turning the

Small Thief

money over in his hands, playing ping pong with it between his palms, flattening the notes and slipping them into his pocket, pulling them out again and waving them like a fan. Finally, he crumpled them into a ball again and placed it back in Hyder's trouser pocket. He stood up and made his way slowly down the corridor.

* * *

Davis's room was tiny: bed, desk, wardrobe, shelves, all interconnected like the living quarters on a submarine. There were no dorms at Harpleton; every boy his own space; a sense of independence and respect, or so the spiel said. As a sixth-former, Davis had the full room version, compared with Hyder's half-walled horsebox. You could do anything when you were walled in: nobody would ever know. Hugh sniffed. Of all the things you can do in a secret space, Davis had devoted himself to the alchemy of smells, the air in his room muggy with evaporated bodily fluids, a choir of orifices singing. He breathed through his mouth, sucking in tiny amounts of air, exhaling quickly. Good, he thought: he didn't want to be here long anyway.

Straight ahead, opposite the door, two wallets sat on Davis's desk: a big, fat wallet, stuffed with notes that Hugh could see from several feet away; and a small, thin wallet that Hugh picked up first. Inside was a single credit card, a few large notes, a business card belonging to someone with the same surname – presumably his father – and a photograph of Davis with his arm around his younger brother, now in his first year at Harpleton, immaculate and untouched for as long as Davis was still at the school. Picking up the other wallet, it was a different beast altogether. Heavy, overstuffed, too large to put in your trouser pocket comfortably – something that would have to be held in a hand or whipped out of a coat pocket. A display wallet, Hugh decided, designed to catch the eye, to be a talking point. And that was what surprised him because, entirely new as he was to this whole way of life, even he knew that financial display wasn't done, except casually. This huge wallet hinted at struggles Davis had himself and at battles he had decided to win through bulk rather than strategy.

From outside, Hugh heard the sounds of the rugby practice in progress. They were too far away from the house, right down the other end of the games pitches, so he couldn't make out what was going on. But he could imagine it, Hyder's tiny frame thrown around as if he was substituting for a missing ball rather than a boy. He wasn't a runner, Hyder.

Hugh snapped open the stud on the fat wallet and extracted a few notes. Then, instead of leaving the room by the door, he opened the window, climbed over the sill and pushed away to jump down onto the grass below. As he did so, the metal catch snagged his new trousers and tore all the way from his groin to his coccyx. He limped across the expanse of grass, holding the material together; through the woods, up the coastal path, back to the village where he used to belong.

ISABEL TEJERA

Exit Interview

Synopsis
Charlie is a 28-year-old wrestling with her lingering attachment to Gaia, her first love. In 2025, faced with the memories of their tumultuous relationship, Charlie devises a daring plan for closure. Madrid's hedonistic Barrio Malasaña – their queer mecca, their fairy drag mother, and their sanctuary of self-expression – becomes the backdrop for their final conversation. Charlie, whose sincerity knows no bounds, clashes with Gaia's stubborn and magnetic persona. As they navigate the fragments of their shared history, Charlie embarks on a soul-searching trip, yearning to unlock the answers that will ultimately allow her to move on.

The narrative swings between the memories of the past and the poignant conversations of the present. In high school, Charlie and Gaia have an obsessive fling – something exciting that they keep from their friends and family. But before they head off to college – Charlie to New England, and Gaia to London – Gaia abruptly ends things, leaving her hurt and bewildered. Determined to move forward, Charlie embraces a new life at Dalvard, befriending the charismatic Rubén and getting entangled with the New York socialite Olympia Van Essen.

Yet, when fate brings Charlie and Gaia face-to-face again during the holidays in Madrid, a destructive cycle of rekindling and separation ensues. Charlie's mental health suffers, affecting her friendships and romantic pursuits. It isn't until she encounters Paloma in a therapist's waiting room that Charlie finds a glimmer of hope. Their long-distance friendship fuels Charlie's vision of a healthier future, one untethered from Gaia.

In the last chapter, present-day Charlie and Gaia agree they've reached their exit. Although her relationship with Gaia may be terminal, Charlie realizes she will always have Malasaña – the pulse of its inexhaustible nightlife will continue to rage in its infinite abundance, in its boundless debauchery, in its pure, queer joy.

Prologue

Word on the street was that God herself made Malasaña hotter than the other barrios, by a few degrees at least, mainly so the tíos and tías could go out at night with nothing but G-strings and riñoneras. Leather and chains were popular in the colder months, as were big wigs and feather boas, but Malasaña in June made even the bears and the cubs, the drag queens and the dykes, the femmes and the butches, los chavales and las chavalas, los maricas and los macarras, all dress down to nothing but their heels and rímel and golden eye shadow.

For Charlie, Malasaña was a beautiful party in hell, where one left behind all pretense of postureo and entered a world unto itself. A place carved with cobblestone streets and terrazas, rainbow flags draped over balconies, sandwich shops and sex stores, tattoo parlors and tapas bars, and alimentaciones on every corner, where one could buy everything from jamón to loose cigarettes to pregnancy tests. These streets told stories. To walk through Malasaña was to walk through time itself, to flip through the pages of history. With its hole-in-the-wall bars that had been there de toda la vida, to its sushi restaurants, art galleries, bookshops, and camera stores, to the mural honoring the late rapper Gata Cattana – one could dip into the 70s, turn the corner into the 90s, and emerge, covered in glitter and grime and God knew what bodily fluids, at an underground techno club.

It was the barrio Charlie had never lived in, but always came to. Having grown up on the outskirts of Madrid, closer to the occasional sheep than any semblance of nightlife, Malasaña was the first urban space she could identify with as a young adult. A queer mecca of sorts. And Malasaña took her in, a fairy drag mother with open arms, saying, *tía, salimos o qué?*

Pues sí, claro que sí.

Chapter 1
December 23rd, 2025

Let us begin with the exit. Years later, they will agree to meet. Charlie will sit under the dim, eggy light of Bar Bulevar on Santa Teresa, in that booth near the colored glass bottles and the cervezas San Miguel. Gaia will arrive late, of course, but Charlie knows this. She will bring a book to pass the time, maybe someone she's covering. When Gaia arrives, they will pause tentatively before hugging. She will look a few years older, laugh lines and worry lines and time spent abroad etched into her eyes. Her hair cut shorter, a late-twenties bob. Gaia will drape a worn leather jacket over the seat. She will go over to the bar and order two Mahous. It will slip her mind that Charlie doesn't drink beer, then she'll remember, just as she places them on the table. Charlie will take small sips, surveying her. She will smile, keep her eyes focused on Gaia – her eyebrows furrowed, listening to Gaia's small talk with that wry smile of hers. Halfway into the first hour, Charlie will be tipsy. She will forget that she doesn't like the acid taste of beer. That she was nervous to come, that she almost didn't show up at all. Gaia will tease her for being such a lightweight. Charlie will hiccup, telling Gaia that she can hold her liquor better than she used to.

"So."

"So."

"Was it about me?"

"What? No, no of course not. It was about me."

Gaia's left hand will hover near Charlie's knee, then retract quietly back into her lap. Charlie will feel a strange tug inside of her, something adjacent to longing but closer to melancholy. And the interview – the one Charlie had always expected, the one she had avoided for a decade, the one she had had with others, but no, not with Gaia, never with Gaia – will begin.

Autumn 2014

The first time Charlie attended Speak-Easy, she and Andrea sat in the back against the wall. They were in one of those small, stuffy classrooms that everyone referred to as Snape's Dungeon – the malodorous freshmen lower floor – and there were barely any chairs left. Charlie recognized some students as the younger siblings of people in her grade but had never interacted with them, seeing as she and Andrea were seniors and most of them were babies, mere 9th and 10th graders. She wondered briefly if it was too late to leave, this was clearly a bad idea, an obvious waste of time – but as she turned to Andrea, Gaia finally arrived, her arms full of books: *The Feminine Mystique* by Betty Friedan, *Play It as It Lays* by Joan Didion, and Charlie made a point of fishing into her backpack for her notebook, a pencil, anything to busy her hands.

Upon Gaia's arrival, the freshmen and sophomores quieted. Gaia splayed the books across the teacher's desk at the front. On cue, someone turned off the lights and the projector went on, with a Powerpoint reading: "Week 3: Representations of Reproductive Rights in Second Wave Feminist Literature."

"OK guys, you know the drill. This is a queer-friendly space. A trans-friendly space. A people of color friendly space. I reserve the right to kick anyone out, if you don't abide by my rules. Straight, cis males to the back – this is your time to shut up."

Charlie glanced at Andrea, suppressing a laugh. She expected some sort of knowing look back, something along the lines of, who does this chula think she is? But Andrea nodded vigorously, captivated by Gaia's words. Never mind that most of the class had no idea what these words meant. Here was Gaia commanding authority, and they were all there to listen. Charlie watched a girl two rows in front of her raise her hand timidly, then lower it, then raise it again when Gaia was looking, trying to capture her attention. The excitement in the room was palpable.

It wasn't always this way, thought Charlie. Ever since kindergarten, she and Gaia had never been in the same group of friends, even though their grade only comprised of sixty-three kids, which meant one collective girl group, one boy group, and a few stray outsiders. Gaia had always been in the latter.

Charlie fit in well at the International School of Madrid. She was the kind of person who joined in on talent shows, varsity sports, student clubs. She got along with the Spanish pijas, the American ex-pats, the international kids who came on rotation with their ambassador parents. She attended pool parties in the summer, went on ski trips to Baqueira in the winter. Andrea had once told her, as she did Charlie's makeup before a party, that she was "pretty, but not in an intimidating way." Charlie – who had struggled with braces and an unfortunate lack of breasts and perpetually noodle-shaped limbs – took this wholly as a compliment.

But ISM was a different place for Gaia: her parents separated early on after her father had an affair with one of the first grade teachers (or so Charlie heard). After a messy divorce covered on the front page of *¡Hola!*, her mother took Gaia's brother, Luca, back to New York, leaving Gaia behind with her father. Mr. Romano was constantly travelling back to Zurich – he was the CEO of Nestlé – and would leave Gaia behind with Esperanza, their trusted nanny from Guatemala. Years later, in the sleepy hours of the night, Gaia would tell Charlie how lost she felt when Esperanza passed away, that she was the only one who always picked Gaia up from the bus stop.

Nobody knew this at the time, though, and the general consensus of the grade was that Gaia was a know-it-all – stuck up, rude, and thought she was better than everyone. Gaia's demeanor encouraged everyone to keep her at arm's length, and often got her sent to the principal's office. One time, in seventh grade, Gaia refused to work on a group science project, and instead opted to do the whole thing by herself. Kids complained when she received perfect marks, saying it was unfair that she hadn't had to work with other people.

But in high school, everything changed. Mr. Romano sent her off to a boarding school in New England for a few years (Andover, Exeter,

Charlie couldn't remember) and when she came back her senior year, Gaia was a different person. She had cut her dirty-blonde hair to her chin, had boobs, and carried herself with an adult sense of confidence. She enamored all the grown-ups: teachers, staff, even the parents. The headmistress gave her permission to start an after-school workshop, Speak-Easy, that centered conversation around things like sex education, feminism, and race. With looming college apps, it was all the hype to join and flex one's newfound wokeness – to fuck the patriarchy, fuck homophobia, and fuck the whole damn system.

This bewildered most of the seniors, especially the españolitos who had been at ISM since they were three. Charlie's friends were your textbook pijos: rich kids of diplomats, bankers. soccer players, even a few distant members of the royal family – the kind with last names like Todos los Santos De Borbón and Primo Rivera de Aragón. Charlie knew of one openly gay girl, Paula, who was the star of the varsity soccer team. She was a tomboy as a kid, and the parents thought it was cute when she acted like one of the boys. But it was very much a don't ask, don't tell situation, and everyone acted surprised when Paula came back after one summer, her hair chopped off like a boy's, and announced she was a Lesbian.

"And that's why Didion's representation of abortion would be problematic by today's standards," explained Gaia. "Any questions?" A few of the kids raised their hands. Next to Charlie, Andrea scribbled something in her notepad, underlining *problematic!!!* several times.

But not everyone approved of Gaia's new authority. Juan and Tomás thought the whole thing was a load of American diarrhea she had imported from the States. They sniggered in the hallways, mocking her in high pitched voices. They drew crude pictures of Gaia in class, ones that, when passed down to Charlie, she would crumple into her backpack. It was a hot, high school mess.

* * *

They had exchanged three words since first grade. Until one day after Speak-Easy, when Gaia followed Charlie into the hallway of Snape's Dungeon and asked her point blank:

"Hey, do you like girls?"

Charlie's face flushed. It was as if someone had crept up behind her and cracked an egg on her head. She reached for her brow. "Huh?"

"I think you're cute," said Gaia. "I was wondering if you liked girls."

Charlie wanted to say something along the lines of, "everybody's a little queer," or "I don't know, but I like you." Something that sounded funny, and witty, and flirty all at once. Something they could joke about later in class, or on a romantic date, or at their wedding. Instead, the afterschool bell rang, and as they got jostled around by sweaty freshmen flooding the hallway, all Charlie could say was:

"I dunno, I guess."

* * *

They would work on college applications, or at least that's what she told her parents. It seemed plausible enough. On the bus over, Charlie kept her legs pressed together, minimizing any accidental skin contact. She looked out the window, resisting the urge to pluck her brow.

Gaia's house was located in one of those historic buildings in Barrio Almagro, the kind with marble columns, a doorman, and an old-fashioned elevator from the pre-Civil War era. Gaia was being quiet, but not in an awkward way. It struck Charlie that she wasn't one for small talk, that she was probably contemplating more important things than how to fill the silence. When they arrived, Gaia brought Charlie up to an open rooftop, where the October sun was staining the sky an alien-like streak of red. Madrid's four skyscrapers sat poised on the horizon, and Charlie listed them to herself in alphabetical order: *Torre Cepsa, Torre de Cristal, Torre Emperador, Torre PwC*. Then she spotted the KIO Towers – Madrid's twin towers – which leaned slightly towards each other, at exactly fifteen degrees, as if sharing a juicy secret about the other buildings. Her parents had taken her there when she was younger, in the hopes she might express an interest in architecture. The interest was still forthcoming.

"This is my prime reading spot," said Gaia finally. They sat down on a large, cotton futon and she pulled out a tin container that had been hidden underneath. "Fumas?"

"No, not really," said Charlie.

Gaia lit one and took a hit, then passed it over. "Just be careful. It's more maría than tobacco. You don't want to burn your throat." Charlie inhaled, then blew out a wispy stream of smoke. She cleared her throat, then took another, bolder hit, and erupted into coughs. They both laughed.

After a few more coughs, Charlie said, "So, is your dad around? Or does he work late, or something?"

"He's in Switzerland for work. His wife lives there too. I'm not sure when he's coming back, maybe next week."

"Huh," said Charlie. "So, who takes care of you, then?"

"Elena does the groceries each week and cleans. So there's not much to do, except go to school and do my work and, like, not get pregnant."

"Huh," said Charlie again. She wondered if Gaia was indeed in a position to get pregnant, and if this was something she, too, should express as an ongoing concern, but instead opted for taking another hit, no coughs this time, and then listing the four skyscrapers in chronological order of when they were completed – *Torre Emperador in 2007, Torre PwC in 2008, Torre de Cristal in 2008, Torre Cepsa in 2009.*

"Hey," said Gaia suddenly. "Can I kiss you?" Charlie looked at her, and before she could say yes, Gaia leaned in. It was gentle, and her breath was warm and slightly tobacco-ish. Charlie felt her insides squirm. Gaia grabbed the back of her neck with one hand and pulled her closer, until they heard, from a distance: "Oye, *guapas!*"

Charlie pulled back. It was one of Gaia's neighbors, catcalling them from the rooftop over. Gaia laughed nervously. "Let's go to my room."

GWEN WILLIAMS

Somewhere to Go

Synopsis
In the run down seaside town of Pantygelyn in the Seventies the paths of two young people cross. **TANWEN** *and* **ELFYN** *are both activists of a sort. Tanwen wants an independent life but has opted to please her parents by her career in social work. Elfyn belongs to a protest movement with an active cell in the village. Over the course of a critical and eventful year their relationship takes both of them forward and helps them to form their own ideas while surviving in the grown up world.*

Tanwen trained in Science. She begins the year feeling that she stuck a pin in a map to decide her next step. But she is a person who questions the obvious and the conventional ideas of others and she wants to be a helpful person. In the absence of any training or supervision she learns from the characters on her caseload – an eccentric family guarded by an eagle, a grieving widower who wears his wife's dresses, teenage runaways and wise vagrants.

Elfyn is an estate agent with strong views about the preservation of his culture and his mother tongue. His perverse strategy is to put off incomers buying second homes by radical and alternative means. He lives in the Yellow Lodge with three other rebels prepared to take non-violent direct action to raise awareness in this divided bicultural community. They admire Greenpeace and Che Guevara and believe in taking responsibility for their actions even if it means prison. Surrounded by spies and saboteurs Elfyn's housemates are wary of his new girlfriend.

At the year's end Tanwen is offered an opportunity to further her career elsewhere but Elfyn has not found a direction yet. Set against a background of division each path will be made by walking.

Somewhere to Go
'Are citizens empowered by these BIG marches and protests? Not at all. All these marches and noise are harmless diversions equivalent to yelling at clouds. No-one in power minds them in the least because they know that none of this energy will ever be directed at anything serious like flood plain zoning, issues with local landfills, local environment activism or de-chartering bad corporations.'

Jim Britell in the Timber Wars

Chapter 1
i

Tanwen came to Pantygelyn because her father told her she must redeem herself. He didn't explain how she was to do this. He said, 'you have to BE somebody.' That was how she had ended up here, dithering in front of the splintered gate of the Belling family house in September.

Sea Crest stood in a parade of three storey houses stoically facing the sea and in the invisible distance was Ireland. In the Victorian era these tall dwellings would have been grand hotels with obedient lawns and flower beds separating them from the sea front and the pebbled beach. Tanwen could see at once that funds were low for the Belling family. She took a breath and put her hand on the gate. Small arrows of rotted wood and flakes of blue paint came off in her quivering fingers as it refused to yield.

In the wilderness of the garden something was unfurling from a tree stump like a ragged brown flag. There had been no mention of an eagle in the paper file of the Belling family. All Tanwen knew was that a small child called Wren lived in the house with blind grandparents and a middle aged self-styled explorer who should never have taken on a baby in the first place. The file said Tom Belling was a 'difficult man' and they were a 'problem family.' She had no idea what that meant and had been putting off this visit hoping that someone in the office would explain. But it was her second week and she was no clearer.

So Tanwen had put on a brave face as usual along with a cherry coloured lipstick to go with her pink hair. Lilac eye shadow to match her shirt dress – the one her father had told her to wear when she went to the interview. The same grey boots which gave her confidence because of the heels.

'Just walk steadily towards me and lift your chin up,' said the man in the paint stained dungarees leaning against the front door. He had been watching her struggle with her motivation and probably thought it entertaining to see her so disconcerted.

'Look straight ahead. Don't act scared and you won't be afraid.'

Under her pale make up Tanwen could feel her face start to glow as she found herself obeying the man. For the first time in weeks someone was offering helpful advice. She shoved the gate and it opened with a crash making the eagle – it really was an eagle – startle up from the tree stump lowering its great flat head. As it prised open a scimitar beak Tanwen felt like prey, but she strode forward on her high heels and fought the urge to turn and run. This whole situation was awkward, this place, this job. Ever since she had left University and signed up in too much haste to this real life she felt as if she had stepped into a cloud and tumbled through a mist wondering where she would land.

Her boss, Mrs Bradley, had dumped a heap of paper files onto her desk and told her to 'try and visit these people soon to show some concern.' It felt like a rebuke. She hadn't grasped what was expected of her except that she was meant to 'solve people's problems.' Mr Lloyd Jones had been driving her around the countryside in his Ford Anglia visiting farms and cottages. Sometimes the 'clients' made him a late breakfast and Tanwen was astonished to see how he made himself at home in other people's houses. These were Social Reviews he explained. He did things by the book. This was her induction.

'Penelope's lunch,' said Tom Belling as Tanwen made it to the porch. She glanced away from the corpses of rabbits suspended from a hook by the door, dripping blood onto the tiled floor. 'Who the hell are you with your big notebook and pale face?'

'Tanwen Price, I'm new at the Area office.' She couldn't bring herself to say 'Social Worker' because – untrained, unqualified, unprepared – she wasn't sure what she was supposed to be.

'Have we seen off Mr Jones then?' Silver wisps of hair sprang up from Tom's eyebrows like question marks giving his eyes the same fierce look as his own eagle.

'He's retiring, Mr Belling, and I'm supposed to replace him.'

'Call me Tom. Great improvement I must say but you look too young. And a city girl straight from college I'm guessing?'

Tanwen forced a smile and remembered she was supposed to befriend this family and perhaps needed to set aside her own ego.

'You're spot on, Mr Belling, Tom. I'm straight from doing a Science degree and not exactly at ease in this job yet but I have to earn my living somehow. I'm wondering what on earth I can do for you, Tom, since you have a Golden Eagle to look after you.'

He laughed. 'But why come here of all places? All the ambitious youngsters are leaving just as you're arriving. You belong in a town with a night club in it.'

'That is where I was until a few weeks ago.'

She had been in the fairyland world of University in England. She was used to laboratory animals – crabs in buckets, water fleas, frogs waiting in tanks to be electrocuted. She had trained pigeons and even taught week old chicks to distinguish between red and blue. Now none of that seemed useful.

Tanwen sighed and changed the subject. 'Until today I had never seen an eagle so close.'

'Penelope's harmless,' said Tom, 'except to rabbits and mice. I brought her back from Kyrgyzstan. Rescued her in fact. She's expecting her lunch right now.'

'Sorry, I should have made an appointment. I can come back....'

'Sod that. We're not appointments people. We're always here. Except when I'm out hunting with Penelope. Come in the house. You want to nag about Wren wagging school I suppose.'

A small half-naked child had joined Tom in the porch and begun to climb up his leg. In the mellow September sun Tanwen felt overdressed.

ii

Elfyn could not forget the day he met Tanwen for the first time. On his way to meet Dan Sayce he had noticed an orange mini with L plates in Market Street doing an emergency stop.

Now he could feel the key to Bryn Glas farm smouldering in his pocket. All through the viewing he'd been trying to dislike the Englishman who wanted the place for breeding horses. Elfyn would prefer a local family to move into the small-holding with young children who would keep the junior school going.

'The widow who lived here, Mrs Jones, let the damp go untreated because she couldn't afford coal,' he told Dan.

'Soon sort that out,' nodded Dan. 'I expected it.'

Elfyn pointed out the leaning chimney, the brambles, the unfriendly neighbours, but Dan was positive these were all soluble problems. He must be very posh, Elfyn decided. This rich boy wouldn't fit in.

A phrase kept reeling around his mind like an earworm. *'Those who would crowd a small window dirty it with their breathing.'* It was a line written in English by a local poet who supported the ideals of their linguistic rights movement.

Despite being prejudiced against Dan, Elfyn had found himself admiring him for his cheerful spirit. Now at the end of the working day he was making his way to the Unicorn to meet his mate Osian – daydreaming. The contradictions buzzed around in his mind. Dan would be an asset to the area. He would bring money. He would stop a rotting small holding from collapsing. Employ local tradesmen maybe.

A shuffling noise made him glance behind him to see if that sneaky figure was still following him. He thought he saw a shadow darting into a shop door as he crossed the High Street and he turned back just in time to see that orange car again. Too late Elfyn heard brakes squeal. It barely touched him he realised later. He was just thrown off balance as he glimpsed the driver, a pale girl with shaggy hair glowing pink in the evening light. Bright birds flashed across his mind. He must have caught his head on something as he fell but it wasn't her fault and instead of pain he felt a rush of cold fire breaking into his veins and he visualised kingfishers burning along a river. He gazed at the driver foolishly not knowing what to expect.

The girl was good at stopping and that was lucky. But no L plates now. Elfyn lying on the ground gave her a thumbs up as she got out of the car and he called out, 'you passed?' She was leaning over him and nodding without smiling.

The stranger had one of those hairstyles he had only seen on TV on models or pop singers – a feathered style short on top and long at the sides. She was not from round here. The backstreet hairdressers of Pantygelyn were too old fashioned to keep up with the new fads. Elfyn was conscious of his own untamed hair and flared trousers. So sixties. And she was so seventies.

iii

'We don't usually get surprise visits from girls with pink hair,' said Tom, being a pony and bouncing the child on his shoulders.

Tanwen followed them into a large room which seemed to be made entirely of bare wood. The echo of their footsteps bounced around the cornices of the high ceiling. The only place to sit was a chapel pew along one wall. A gigantic Welsh dresser was loaded with jars and tins of food and somewhere in the house onions were being boiled.

Tom lowered Wren to the floor where she picked up a plastic headless doll. Tanwen decided she must first connect with the child to gain the father's good opinion. 'I'd put the kettle on,' shouted Tom from the next room, 'but I've just noticed we're out of milk. We've plenty of lager though.'

Tanwen crouched on the floor with the child. 'So you're Wren?' The girl nodded in an intense way as if she couldn't speak. She gazed at Tanwen as she might stare at an alien. 'Miss Pink, you are,' said Wren.

iv

Tanwen had abandoned the estate agent in the street. The collision had been his own fault, she decided. He'd been dawdling and loosening his tie and glancing over his shoulder all at once.

She wasn't clear about what happened – only that she'd performed a sharper emergency stop than in her driving test that morning in the middle of Market Street. Then she was leaning over the guy and he was definitely conscious because she was replying to his question. 'It was my fourth time,' she remembered saying and noticed his eyes were a heroic green and a line of blood streaked his temple. She wondered if he might be yet another person to be wary of – a Welshman like her father with old fashioned values. The rest of the estate agent was fairly neutral. A grey suit that looked as if his mother had made him buy it for a cousin's wedding but at least he wore it as if he hated restrictions.

She dabbed at the blood with her father's man-sized check hankie. In the last few days she had often wept into this scrap of sympathetic cotton. 'It's a scratch,' she heard him say. 'I caught it as I fell and no harm done.' But as he scrambled to his feet he staggered and she grabbed his arm. They performed an unsteady salsa in the middle of the street as they both struggled to regain their balance. 'I was on my way to that pub,' said Elfyn, pointing to the Unicorn. 'You look pale. We should both have a brandy for the shock.'

Tanwen shook her head. She'd had enough for one day after the driving test, the shock of passing it, being left alone in this place, the uncertainty about the job starting the next day, having to turn up at an office and meet other people who probably knew what they were doing. And she still had to search for her lodgings with a Methodist friend of her Dad's. She was dreading it. She'd had enough of that type of person as a child. And she mustn't drink brandy or lager while she had the mini.

'If you're sure you're OK I need to go. Something to do.' The last thing she wanted right now was to have a drink with some local chap who seemed to be in a reverie.

'What's your badge?' she asked.

'Oh that. It says Cymraeg Gyntaf. Welsh First it means in English'

'I know. I can read. But you spoke to me in English first. Why? I would have understood you in Welsh.'

Biographies

Judge's biography

Sarah Hall was born and lives in Cumbria. She is the author of six novels and three short story collections. She has won multiple literary prizes in the UK and overseas, including the BBC National Short Story Award twice, the Portico, Edge Hill and Commonwealth Prizes, and the EM Forster Award. She's been shortlisted for the Booker prize and the Prix Femina Etranger, and was on the Granta Best Young British Novelists list in 2013. She is Professor of Practice at the University of Cumbria, patron of Humanists UK, and a Fellow of the RSL.

Writers' biographies

Jilly Carrell was originally from Edinburgh and is now from everywhere. 18 years as an army wife, her husband's six tours of Afghanistan, and the impact of the conflict on military families, provides the inspiration for her first novel, *The Origins of Poppies*. After his death during lockdown, she paused for a year to mother her daughters and write her way through everything. In 2023, she graduated with an MA (distinction) in Creative Writing from Bath Spa. This Autumn, she will start her PhD at the University of Winchester, where she now lives with her two daughters, four dogs and rescue cats.

P C Cubitt is the English author of the novel *Fly Catcher*. She is an Africanist scholar and (as Christine Cubitt) has been a contributor and editor to a number of academic journals. Her PhD on the international peace-building mission in Sierra Leone was published by Routledge. Christine's recent move to fiction was inspired by her work in Africa and she is currently working on her second novel. She is the mother of three grown-up sons and lives with her husband in Yorkshire. Find her at pccubitt.com

Pauline Diamond Salim works for a human rights charity in Glasgow. She is an ex-journalist and wrote for UK newspapers and magazines before moving into the charity sector. For the last ten years she has worked for a refugee agency that supports people seeking safety in Scotland. Her second novel, *I Just Live Here*, was shortlisted for the 2023

Caledonia Novel Award and the 2023 Scottish Book Trust New Writers Award.

Lucy Foster is a writer and teacher living in Cornwall. She has a PhD from Cambridge University in the cultural history, art and literature of the Mexican coastline, and teaches there on Latin American papers for the Modern Languages Department. Lucy has worked in editorial at Sceptre, Hodder and Stoughton, as a translator from French and Spanish, a literary scout and, before all that, as a cabaret dancer in a fishing town in Mexico. She recently founded a community art collective on the Mexican west coast, @salonxaltemba on Instagram.

Faiza Hasan worked as a journalist, trained as a chef from Cordon Bleu, ran a pop-up restaurant and an online macaroon shop in London until a life changing diagnosis of Fibromyalgia returned her to her first love, writing. She has an MA in Journalism from Stanford University, an MA in Creative Writing from Cambridge University and has attended the Bread Loaf Writers Conference. Her short stories have been short and longlisted in competitions, including third place at the Bristol Prize, 2020, and her novel has been longlisted for The Yeovil Prize, Pontas Emerging Writers and TLC Pen Factor.
Twitter:@paandaan, @thetatteredcovers

David Hill is a Scottish author, currently based in England, whose work combines fiction and art history. A graduate of Durham University and Edinburgh University's Creative Writing Programme (MA Distinction), he is currently completing an MA in Art History from Birkbeck College, University of London. His academic research and fiction writing both seek to explore feminist reassessments of canonical artworks, which were exploitative in their production. He also runs an award-winning bespoke jewellery business. You can find him on Instagram, Threads or Twitter @1_davidhill.

Hilary Hudgins is a New York writer who moved to Norwich to pursue a Masters in Creative Writing at the University of East Anglia but stayed because she found life not only much calmer, but also, oddly, less lonely. She is interested in how fiction can explore the subjectivity of how we interact with one another while highlighting the choices people so often make to dwell on perceived differences. Hilary lives with her partner, Niko, and their evolutionary misstep of a dog, Enzo. When not writing, she's usually cooking. hilaryhudgins.com

Biographies

Angela Hunter is a professor of French literature – at least, that's what was supposed to happen. The PhD dream long since abandoned but her love of the written word intact, she writes in the hours not needed for work and trying to raise two good humans. She is interested in the characters who don't fit, the families that don't function and the homes that don't shelter. *A Scrape of Patience* is her first novel; the second is percolating. Angela studied a Masters in language and literature in Glasgow where she grew up. She lives in Chester with her family.

Tony Irvin has a veterinary degree and PhD from Cambridge and went to Kenya for twenty years, to study a disease of cattle and wildlife which no one outside Africa has ever heard of. He travelled throughout the region working in collaboration with African scientists and indigenous people, such as the Maasai. He has published widely in the field of scientific literature but, having returned to the UK, now writes fiction for adults and children, all of which is set in hot places. He has been shortlisted the H E Bates Centenary Award, and the Wells Festival of Literature Children's Award.

Jenny Jack is originally from Fife, and studied medicine in Edinburgh, where a fascination with patients' stories led her to specialise in psychiatry. After further training in London and Oxford, she now lives on the edge of the Peak District with her partner and three children, working as a consultant psychiatrist in a service for Early Intervention in Psychosis. Her writing is inspired by her work and by an interest in folktales, mythology and elements of magical realism. She has an MPhil in Writing, has published various pieces of short fiction and been shortlisted in the Off the Shelf Sheffield Short Story Competition.

SallyAnne Khan boarded at school. She has always had a problem with reading because so much of it was a required to keep her entertained. If they had given her a room full of drums, it might not have taken her so long to get around to writing. *Bem's Dream War* is her first novel. It is a joust with the phooey we are told every day and imagines what might happen if we actually had the backbone to confront it. She lives in central London and spends most of her working life in visual arts.

Rebekah Miron is a Freelance Writer and Editor from the South West of England who not-so-secretly would rather be working on her own books. She was awarded a Distinction and the Kate Bertram Prize for her Master's work in Creative Writing at Lucy Cavendish College, University of Cambridge. Her poetry has been broadcast internationally and published both online and in print, featuring in *The Emma Press Anthology of Illness* and shortlisted in The Frogmore Poetry Prize in 2020. She started writing her novel, *Love, I must go*, in January of 2023. Twitter: @rebekahmiron

Murungu is a teacher and storyteller born in Zimbabwe and living in the UK. *HuKaMa*, his first novel, explores comradeship amongst African street kids. People don't notice street kids. And yet they live, love and laugh. *And are murdered for witchcraft*. Based on appalling truth, *HuKaMa* offers a story of hopeful, tender redemption. And a spotlight on deep corruption. His next book, a comedy, is based on international film experience and reveals the antics of companies trying to save the world. Featuring Sharon Stone, Richard Chamberlain, Danny Glover, the BBC.

Yoanna Pak is a London-based Canadian. She moved to London after working retail in Paris and teaching secondary school in Seoul, South Korea. Her writing career began when she applied to the MA in Creative Writing programme at Goldsmiths College to avoid deportation back to Canada. *Wolnam*, her first novel, was born at Goldsmiths. Its beginning chapters were shortlisted for the Pat Kavanagh Prize. *Wolnam* has been shortlisted for the SI Leeds Literary Prize and longlisted for the Virginia Prize for Fiction. A husband and two children later, she hopes to publish *Wolnam* and finally finish her PhD.

Susan Perry was born in Suffolk. She spent many years working in communications as a writer and editor across print and electronic media in London, Chicago and Cape Town, before returning to the UK to concentrate on writing fiction full time. She has an MA (with distinction) in Creative Writing from the University of Cape Town and several years of editorial and mentoring experience through her work with a local writing group in Cambridge, where she now resides. She is fascinated by the theme of 'outsiders' and is currently working on her second novel around this topic.

Caroline Price read music at York University and after working as a violinist and teacher in Glasgow, London and Kent, she has now settled in East Anglia where her family lives. Writing has been as important to her as music: she has published four collections of poetry, and her poems and stories have appeared widely in literary publications and been awarded many prizes, including twice in the Bridport Prize. Her passion for the French language and culture led to a diploma in French through the Open University, and France has provided inspiration for the two novels she's currently working on.

Biographies

Margaret Sessa-Hawkins is a producer with the BBC's Audio Science unit in Cardiff, currently helming Unexpected Elements, a popular-science show airing on the World Service. Born in the United States, most of her adult life has been split between Malawi, Britain, and America. *Migratory Patterns,* her first novel, was completed as part of her PhD thesis in Creative Writing at the University of East Anglia. She is currently working on a second novel about a detective agency investigating corporate crimes — fueling her writing with a slightly unhealthy combination of digestives, Welsh cakes, and loose-leaf teas.

Liz Skitt grew up in a remote village in Scotland, which was beautiful but probably propelled her to escape into books and travel as soon as she could. Like her main character in *Small Thief*, she lived in the eastern part of Germany shortly after the Berlin Wall came down and in Argentina in the early 2000s. Professionally, Liz is director of training and change management at an international company. She started *Small Thief* at the Faber Academy Writing a Novel Course. She is now working on a series of ghost stories set in various countries she has lived in.

Isabel Tejera grew up in Madrid, Spain and has also lived in Andover, MA, Providence, RI, New York, Oxford and East London. A broadcast journalist with a background in conflict and international relations, she has a BA from Brown and a Masters from the University of Oxford. Her media experience spans CNN International, VICE World News, and her current role at CNBC. Her debut work, *Exit Interview*, is a queer, coming-of-age novel inspired by her multicultural upbringing between Madrid and the US. She is currently a student at Faber Academy.

Gwen Williams lives in Wales. She has a background in Social Work and a Masters Degree in Art and Psychotherapy. Inspiration for *Somewhere to Go* came during lockdown when she was invited to contribute to *Merched Peryglus (Dangerous Women)*, an anthology which celebrates the role of daring women activists during the successful, but ongoing, campaign for Welsh linguistic rights. It will be published this year by Honno. To date, three of her poems and a story have been shortlisted in the Bridport Competition. She is one of four resident artists at Ladder Store Studios in Llandudno. Instagram @laddercymru; @gwenwilliamsartist